AMERICAN
MASTERWORKS

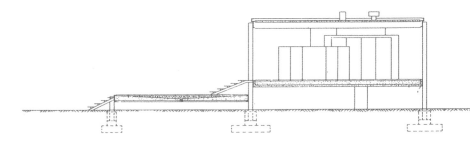

AMERICAN MASTERWORKS

HOUSES OF THE 20TH AND 21ST CENTURIES

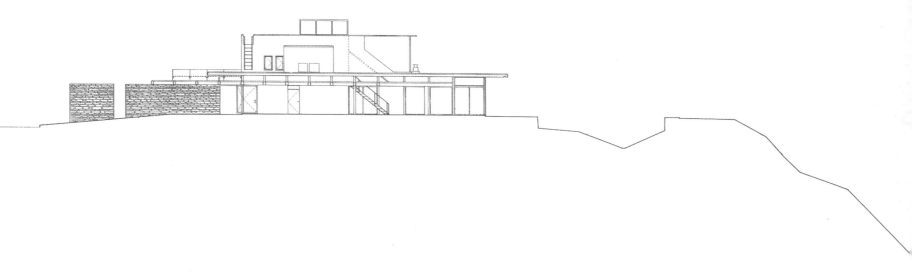

EDITED BY KENNETH FRAMPTON AND DAVID LARKIN
TEXT BY KENNETH FRAMPTON

RIZZOLI
NEW YORK

The authors and Rizzoli International Publications, Inc. are extremely
grateful for the extraordinary cooperation of the owners of the
buildings illustrated in this book.

Kenneth Frampton wishes to acknowledge the assistance he
received during the preparation of the first and second editions from
Jori Erdman, Karen Melk, Joseph Rosa, Michael Delfausse, and
Duygu Demir.

Reprint copyright 2008 by
RIZZOLI INTERNATIONAL PUBLICATIONS, INC.
300 Park Avenue South
New York, New York 10010
www.rizzoliusa.com

First published in the United States of America in 1995

Copyright © 1995, 2008 Rizzoli International Publications, Inc.,
David Larkin, and Kenneth Frampton

2008 2009 2010 2011 / 10 9 8 7 6 5 4 3 2 1

ISBN 10: 0-8478-3146-9
ISBN 13: 978-0-8478-3146-3

Library of Congress Cataloging-in-Publication Data

Frampton, Kenneth.
  American masterworks : houses of the 20th and 21st centuries /
edited by Kenneth Frampton and David Larkin ; text by Kenneth
Frampton. -- Rev. ed.
      p. cm.
  Includes bibliographical references.
  ISBN 978-0-8478-3146-3 (hardcover)
  1. Architecture, Domestic--United States. 2. Architecture--United
States--20th century. 3. Architecture--United States--21st century.
I. Larkin, David, 1936- II. Title.
  NA7208.F67 2008
  728'.3709730904--dc22
                        2008022084

Printed in China

AMERICAN MASTERWORKS

A HOUSE I know is but a temporary abode, but how delightful it is to find one that has harmonious proportions and a pleasant atmosphere. One feels somehow that even moonlight, when it shines into the quiet domicile of a person of taste, is more affecting than elsewhere. A house, though it may not be in the current fashion or elaborately decorated, will appeal to us by its unassuming beauty; a grove of trees with an indefinably ancient look; a garden where plants, growing of their own accord, have a special charm; a veranda and an open-work wooden fence of interesting construction; and a few personal effects left carelessly lying about, giving the place an air of having been lived in. A house which multitudes of workmen have polished with every care, where strange and rare Chinese and Japanese furnishings are displayed, and even the grass and trees of the garden have been trained unnaturally, is ugly to look at and most depressing. How could anyone live for long in such a place? The most casual glance will suggest how likely such a house is to turn in a moment to smoke.

—YOSHIDA KENKO *Essays in Idleness,* 1328

THE MODERN AMERICAN HOUSE REVISITED

PREFACE TO THE SECOND EDITION

Thirteen years have elapsed since the first edition of *American Masterworks*, and now, following our entry into another century, it seemed an opportune moment to return to the topic and produce a second, revised and enlarged edition bringing the coverage of the anthology closer to the present.

The passage of time has not made the task of selection any easier for as with every anthology there is always the intractable issue as to the criteria on the basis of which one decides to include certain works and exclude others. The selection was not made any easier both with the considerable number of remarkable houses realized in the United States since 1992, the date of Steven Holl's Stretto House with which the first edition ends. In fact, instead of an expanded second edition, one could have easily produced a second volume of approximately the same length as the first, running from the early 1990s to 2008.

In the end we opted for enlarging the first edition by adding eleven houses among which was Henry Hobson Richardson's renowned Glessner House, completed posthumously in Chicago in 1887. This effectively pushed the beginning of a self-consciously modern domesticity back in time, with the result that the anthology now extends beyond the span of the twentieth century at both ends. This in effect takes us closer to the span of the first synoptic overview, 1869–1929, that is Lewis Mumford's Brown Decades, the title of his first book of 1926.

Aside from the Alan IW Frank House realized in Pittsburgh, Pennsylvania, in 1939, and the only too canonical Kaufmann House built in Palm Springs in 1946, both glaring omissions from the first edition, the remaining additional exemplars have been taken from the last fifteen years of production.

For the rest this anthology remains only slightly altered, since as before all the houses were realized within the borders of the United States and are hence both American and modern, notwithstanding the fact that the very first house featured in the collection is now one hundred and twenty years old. This makes the qualification modern even more debatable given the ever quickening pace of fashionable taste, since what is modern for one generation will not be regarded as such by the next and so on. Despite such high-style fluctuations, there is still obviously something that we may call the typical American house, which may be found with minor variations throughout the country. This typical builder's residence has

changed so little over the last fifty years that, statistically speaking, it may be regarded as the quintessential American home. Needless to say this type will not be found here. How, then, have we construed the concept of "modernity" for the purposes of deciding which houses to include? Aside from the national boundary, certain other parameters were established— above all, the fact that the houses had to be represented by new photographs taken specially for the publication, which meant, of course, that the houses had to be extant and in the main still occupied. Here and there we made exceptions, where a house was being restored or where it was otherwise unavailable, in which case we have used existing images.

Apart from this, the modern house that we have attempted to represent had to meet other criteria, some more objective than others. Each example has been designed by architects of high caliber, although this has not prevented us from featuring the work of relatively young architects. Second, each house may be said to possess a certain level of complexity and poetic depth. This will no doubt be regarded as the most subjective criterion, since it has led to the exclusion of certain canonical, almost mythic modern houses, which were omitted because they were seen as lacking in semantic density. However, this prejudice did not prevent us from including other extremely simple houses whose poetic complexity lay in their material precision and tectonic articulation, as in Philip Johnson's renowned Glass House.

We wanted to trace the evolution of certain cultural images or values as these have been incorporated into modern American house design. We began with the Gamble House by Greene and Greene, as a well-preserved example of the California arts and crafts style at the turn of the century. This house may be seen as an heir to the Shingle Style houses of the 1880s, which have been generally regarded as the progenitors of domestic modernity in America.

We went on to show the scope of Frank Lloyd Wright's influence on the American house throughout the twentieth century, not only in respect of the changing character of his own work as this appears in the Storer and Sturges houses and in Fallingwater, but also in terms of his influence on his assistants Rudolph Schindler and Richard Neutra. This trajectory led us to treat the rich legacy of the Southern California School as it has passed from Charles Eames at mid-century through Craig Ellwood down to more recent California architects such as Peter de Bretteville.

It is hard to trace a corresponding continuity in the South or on the East Coast, where both the established bourgeoisie and the nouveau riche were all but exclusively committed to neocolonial and other pastiche expressions, particularly during the first three decades of the century. Thus they initially failed to embrace either the form or the lifestyle of the liberated modern house.

In general this inhibiting climate also prevailed in the Midwest, despite Wright's efforts and the triumph of the Prairie Style in and around Chicago at the turn of the century. Indeed one can only conclude that Wright's clientele were particularly exceptional in terms of their self-confidence and cultivation. One need only visit the interior of the Francis W. Little House of 1913 as it is now installed in the Metropolitan Museum of Art in New York to sense this. This class lived in their Wrightian houses like secular princes, with a fastidiousness that recalls the Prussian nobility of the early nineteenth century. In this respect, the modern American house has always manifested an intense drive for self-fulfillment. At its best it has been a testament of hope, both for the individual and for the nation, particularly in its effort to move beyond the confining traditions of the Old World.

The emigré architects who arrived in the United States throughout the latter half of the 1930s did much to change the taste of the East Coast establishment. This shift in received taste, as it were, was presaged by the International Style exhibition staged at the Museum of Modern Art in 1931 under the joint curatorship of Alfred Barr, Philip Johnson, and Henry-Russell Hitchcock. This exhibition effectively prepared the ground for figures like Walter Gropius, Mies van der Rohe, and Marcel Breuer to migrate to the States and thereafter to assume positions of prominence within both the architecture schools and the profession. In general we have tried to capture the work of this generation although there are a number of gaps: above all, there is no house by Breuer, aside from his collaboration with Gropius on two houses: Gropius's own house in Lincoln, Massachusetts (1937) and the Frank House in Pittsburgh (1939). The modern flourished on the West Coast during the 1930s and 1940s, above all in the houses designed and realized under the auspices of John Entenza's Case Study program.

The militant "tradition of the new" returned to the East Coast in the mid-1960s, most notably with the emergence of the so-called New York Five: Peter Eisenman, Michael Graves, Charles Gwathmey, John Hedjuk, and Richard Meier. These "white architects" entered into an ongoing debate with the "grays," who included the more prominent members of the Kahnian Philadelphia School, above all, Charles Moore, Robert Venturi, and Romaldo Giurgola. This softer, more populist American modernity was critically sustained by the opinions and the influential writings of Robert Stern and Vincent Scully. My own prejudice in this regard is surely evident from the fact that I have included more works by "whites" than "grays" in this anthology.

Distancing ourselves from such regional, factional issues, we have also opted to feature the California work of Ricardo Legorreta and Frank Gehry who, in various ways, have introduced a totally new discourse into the American domestic scene.

The last twenty-eight years have seen the emergence of completely different influences and the rising work of a younger generation that has elected to continue and augment various strands of the American domestic tradition as it has been advanced during the course of this century. Thus Mark Mack and Steven Holl exhibit somewhat different versions of an expression which Mack has labeled neo-primitivism with Mack owing much to Adolf Loos and Holl being somewhat closer to Carlo Scarpa. The Mexican master architect Luis Barragán has also influenced the work of this generation as is evident in Mack's recent houses and above all in those designed by the San Francisco architect Stanley Saitowitz, whose De Napoli House is a tour de force in this regard.

The other extension of the modern tradition still evident in the best recent American work is a line that combines Miesianism with the productive modularity of the Case Study houses, with something of the formal rigor initially brought to the American scene by the New York Five. Among such works particular note should now be taken not only of Ron Krueck's neo-Miesian, ferro-vitreous courtyard house built in Chicago in 1980 but also of Michael Bell's equally neo-Miesian glass house, realized at Ghent, New York, in 2007.

One of the most contentious issues inadvertently raised by this anthology is the question of the appropriate boundary separating architecture from fine art. This question may be bluntly elaborated as follows: Are houses to be regarded as an occasion for the creation of art, as though they were nothing more than giant pieces of inhabited sculpture, or should they be construed as action settings that first and foremost must provide for appropriately inflected environments, conducive to their felicitous occupation and use? This issue turns on the term *appropriate* and the way in which this may be determined in part through the poesis with which the micro-space has been detailed and in part through the way in which the overall dwelling represents a particular vision of the world. Such issues are perhaps raised with the greatest urgency by the extremely aestheticized houses designed by such architects as Frank Gehry, Eric Own Moss, Frank Israel, and Thom Mayne. Meanwhile on the East Coast, Simon Ungers and Tom Kinslow turn in a completely opposite direction, that is to say toward a cryptic, T-shaped sign in core-ten steel (opposite), standing stark in the upstate New York landscape as the ultimate uncompromising gesture in rendering the house a work of art.

—Kenneth Frampton, March 2008

8

FROM THE BROWN DECADES
TO THE FRAGMENTED METROPOLIS

1869–1929

Influenced by Orson Fowler's thesis of 1848, setting forth the ergonomic advantages of the octagonal house, Catherine Beecher Stowe's *The American Woman's Home* of 1869 effectively inaugurated the household reform movement in America. This book was the first attempt to rationalize the kitchen by recommending continuous work surfaces and convenient storage. Such initiatives were developed further in E. C. Gardener's *Houses and How to Make Them* (1876) and Christine Frederick's *Household Engineering: Scientific Management in the Home* (1915). During the same period, the prosperous middle class that emerged in the Northeast after the Civil War was demanding a new type of vacation dwelling. This relaxed modus vivendi, based stylistically on the Queen Anne manner of Richard Norman Shaw, was crystallized into the Shingle Style by Henry Hobson Richardson in the early 1870s. This style acquired its definitive format in H. H. Richardson's Watts Sherman House, completed in Newport, Rhode Island, in 1874. As Vincent Scully has written:

It was Henry Hobson Richardson who first brought the inherent American instinct toward continuity into union with the equally inherent and constantly growing desire for permanence and security. His Watts Sherman House of 1874 smoothed over the mid-century expression of the skeleton. It stretched the late medieval–early Renaissance elements of contemporary English work into horizontally extended window screens, cutting through the big gable that sought to contain them. By the early eighties Richardson and many other architects had transformed influences from early American colonial architecture itself into thin shingled skins of wall, tightly stretched by the pressure of continuously open spaces inside them and engulfing exterior spaces of porches into their volumes. Continuity and permanent shelter were thus united in a single theme.[1]

1.

Richardson's Shingle Style houses, such as the Hay House in Washington, D.C., and Paine House in Waltham, Massachusetts, both of 1886, developed open plans that centered about highly theatrical stair halls (fig. 1). Henry-Russell Hitchcock has written of the Paine House:

[The stairs] pour down into the room like a mountain cataract, and even the turned spindles of the balustrades and the small square panels look well seen against the light for the lack of light in the room is not altogether unfortunate. The brown woodwork, with the orange-red plaster wall stencilled with great Japanese symbols, forms a rich harmony beneath the great structural beams of the ceiling.[2]

The American penchant for the Orient came to the fore in the early work of Frank Lloyd Wright and continued, as it moved west to California (and thus closer to Japan), to blossom forth in the Japanesque work of Greene and Greene in Pasadena. However, as Lewis Mumford reminds us in his book *The Brown Decades*, we may not dispense with Richardson quite so readily, at least not until we have acknowledged

11

his last domestic work of consequence, the monumental Glessner House in Chicago, built of dressed stone and featuring a radical L-shaped plan edged up against the street (fig. 2). This introspective courtyard form, closed toward the exterior, will reappear in all its fullness in Frank Lloyd Wright's Usonian house type of the 1930s.

It would be difficult to overestimate Wright's seminal contribution to the development of the modern American house, particularly during the affluent period from the late nineteenth century to the crash of 1929. Yet despite his brilliance, Wright's renowned Prairie

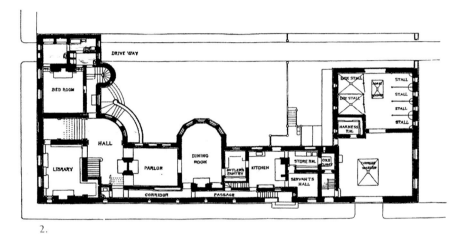

2.

Style would have been unthinkable without the pioneering example of Richardson and the other talented Shingle Style architects, notably Stanford White, Wilson Eyre, and above all Bruce Price. Scully has identified Price's Kent House in Tuxedo Park, New York, of 1886, as lying behind the first stage of Wright's Oak Park residence, built in that rising Chicago suburb in 1889. The long-standing American practice of locating the fireplace and chimney in the center of the house attained its full space-making potential in these key works by Price and Wright. The planning strategy was similar, for both men arranged their rooms to rotate about a central chimney and an adjacent stair. In addition they provided a generous veranda that guaranteed, as it were, a certain lateral continuity to the internal space.

Wright's subsequent expansion of his domestic format by simultaneously increasing the horizontal dimension and elevating the apparent height of the house first appears in the Winslow House,

12

3.

River Forest, Illinois (1893, fig. 3) and emerged even more forcibly in the ingeniously planned Richardsonian McAfee House of the following year. Wright monumentalized both by raising the apparent height of the ground floor through a stringcourse running beneath the upper window sills. This horizontal stress, reinforced by unbroken eaves and by equally horizontal outriding walls, reappears in the Ward Willits House built in Highland Park, Illinois, in 1902. The latter, Wright's most abstract house of the time, effectively crystallized the Prairie Style, largely through consolidating fenestration into strips of casement windows. Here, as never before, the internal space pinwheels around the central stair and chimney, while outriding walls and low-hipped roofs, carried on massive piers, expand the house into the garden. Like the slightly earlier Hickock House at Kankakee, Illinois, the Ward Willits residence features eaves and stringcourses executed in dark wooden trim, in strong contrast to its white walls. As Grant Carpenter Manson has noted, the Japanese aura of these houses may well reflect Wright's familiarity with the Ho-o-den Temple, built by the Japanese government for the Chicago World's Columbian Exposition of 1893.

If we assume that actual confrontation with a Japanese building was the necessary mechanism at a certain juncture in his career to give those concepts reality and direction, then many steps in the evolution of his architecture can be rationally explained. As examples: the translation of the tokonama, the permanent element of a Japanese interior and the focus of domestic contemplation and ceremony, into its Western counterpart, the fireplace, but a fireplace raised to unprecedented animistic importance; the frank revelation of the masonry of the fireplace and chimney, the one desired solid substance in an architecture of ever-increasing movement; the opening out of interior spaces away from the chimney toward shifting planes of glass at their further limits; the extension of the great eaves beyond these planes to modify and control the intensity of the light which they admit and to protect them from the weather; the subdivision of the interior space by suggesting rather than partition, acknowledging and accommodating the fluctuating human uses to which it is put; the elimination of all sculptured and varnished trim in favour of flat surfaces and natural wood—all these and more could have been adduced from the lesson of the Ho-o-den.[3]

The emergence of the Prairie Style coincided with Wright's theoretical maturity, as demonstrated in his famous lecture "The Art and Craft of the Machine," delivered at Jane Addams's Hull House Settlement in Chicago in 1901. Taking as his point of departure his youthful despair on reading *Notre Dame de Paris*, in which Victor Hugo concluded that printing would eventually eliminate architecture, Wright countered with the thesis that the machine, if intelligently used, could become an agent for abstraction and purification, thereby saving built form from the ravages of industrialization.

Wright's Prairie Style attained its domestic apotheosis in three canonical houses: the Darwin D. Martin House, Buffalo, New York (1904); the Avery Coonley House, Riverside, Illinois (1908); and the Robie House, Chicago (1909, figs. 4 & 5). The latter's precise yet

4.

emblematic plan bestowed an unsurpassed simplicity and elegance, making it into the ideal image of the modern house for many years to come. The Robie House already embodied almost all of the principles of Wright's domestic agenda, as he would belatedly summarize this in his nine-point manifesto of 1931; that is to say, the reduction of the number rooms of a dwelling to a minimum; the integration of the building into its site; the elimination of the cellular plan in favor of free-flowing space; the replacement of the basement by a podium; the unification of the interior with the exterior; the substitution of multiple materials by one material; the integration of mechanical services and furniture as much as possible; and, finally, the suppression of all applied decoration.[4]

Significantly enough, the Prairie Style ethos gravitated west rather than east in two stages, appearing first in the pioneering arts and crafts bungalow manner evolved by the Greene brothers during their

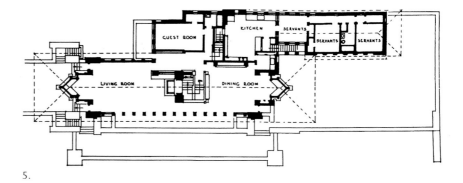

5.

Pasadena practice prior to the popularization of the Spanish colonial style by Bertram Goodhue through his San Diego Pan-Pacific Exhibition of 1915. It surfaced again, a few years later, as a transformed style, in Wright's Hollyhock House, realized for Aline Barnsdall on Olive Hill, Los Angeles, between 1916 and 1921.

Hollyhock represents a major break in Wright's development in that he moved away from the open, screenlike walls and roofs of his midwestern manner toward a monumental "desert style" patently influenced by pre-Columbian architecture. Painstakingly assembled out of concrete-blocks and fake plaster-work on timber framing and trusses, Hollyhock aspired to a constructional method and mode that Wright eventually achieved with his textile-block houses of the 1920s. Wright used concrete block for the first time in the Millard House, otherwise known as La Miniatura, built in Pasadena in 1923. Looking back on this development, Wright wrote in 1932:

The concrete block? The cheapest (and ugliest thing) in the building world. It lived mostly in the architectural gutter as an imitation of rock face stone. Why not see what could be done with that gutter rat? Steel wedded to it cast inside the joints and the block itself brought into some broad, practical scheme of general treatment; then why would it not be fit for a phase of modern architecture? It might be permanent, noble, beautiful.

It would be cheap. I finally had found a simple mechanical means to produce a complete building that looks the way the machine made it, as much at least, as any fabric need look. Tough, light, but not thin; imperishable; plastic; no necessary lie about it anywhere and yet machine-made, mechanically perfect. Standardization as the soul of the machine here for the first time may be seen in the hand of the architect, put squarely up to the limitations of imagination, the only limitation of building.[5]

As cubic as Wright's Unity Temple of 1904, the Millard House developed its internal volume inward, outward, and upward at the same time. The somber thick-wall layering of the space was relieved by the patterned surfaces of the textile block, by the filtered light they admit to the interior and by the luxurious planting that surrounded the house on every side.

With its patterned, perforated glass-filled apertures, La Miniatura embodied the essential syntax of a system Wright would employ, with subtle variations, in three subsequent Los Angeles dwellings: the Freeman, Storer, and Ennis houses. With the exception of the Freeman residence, where the blocks run into open glass corners and the muntins seem to extend the mortar joints between the blocks, Wright's subsequent California block houses add little to the basic Millard syntax. Except for this prototype, in which the units were cast from wooden molds, the later textile blocks were invariably made from metal patterns filled with a dry, compacted concrete mix. The blocks were wet-cured for ten days prior to assembly, then laid in a stack-bond pattern with wire reinforcement between the horizontal and vertical joints. Wherever possible Wright introduced decomposed granite from the site into the mix so as to achieve an intrinsic, not to say mystical, union between nature and culture; however, this inadvertent incorporation of organic matter proved detrimental to the durability of the construction.

Wright employed three basic patterns in his blocks—radially symmetrical, symmetrical, and asymmetrical—irrespective of whether they were simply indented, perforated, or filled with glass. This variation, plus the different degrees of permeability, afforded a wide range of alternatives with which to express different surface conditions and to vary the superficial rhythm and scale of the overall mass. In the Millard House, Wright attempted to solve all of the different junction conditions with a single block. He thus conceived of built-up columns and piers as special cases to be integrated into the overall system. In the event, however, it was often quite difficult to repeat the same standard element, as we may induce from the Freeman House, where 40 percent of the blocks are mitered at the corners.

Wright erected his last concrete-block house in 1929 in Tulsa, Oklahoma, for his cousin Richard Lloyd Jones. In retrospect, it appears to have been a transitional work, since Wright abandoned the hitherto finely woven fabric of the square textile block in favor of larger rectangular units, laid up as walls or monumental piers. Wright relinquished his unrealizable ideal of a building without

windows, creating an alternating pattern of wide piers and glazed vertical slots of the same width, with solid and void equally matched. This passage from the sixteen-inch-square pattern of the Los Angeles houses to a fifteen-by-twenty-inch, plain-faced, stack-bonded block pattern produced a paradoxical decrease in apparent mass, the scale being diminished through suppressing floor heights. Apart from permitting a consistent alignment between block courses and window transoms, the larger block had other advantages, from the labor saved in the actual laying to the filling of the hollow cores with substantial amounts of cement and steel reinforcement to produce integrated reinforced-concrete piers of greater strength and simplicity. Alternatively, similar voids could accommodate conduits, ventilation ducts, and piped services.

Wright's emigré apprentices, Rudolph Schindler and Richard Neutra, took the Prairie Style to California. Schindler worked for Wright in Chicago before moving to Los Angeles in 1919 to supervise the construction of the Hollyhock House. Since Wright was away in Japan at the time, Schindler was effectively given a free hand to elaborate the general concept in Wright's name. Thus Schindler came to be largely responsible for two houses on the property, the Director's House built in 1920 and Residence B, designed for Aline Barnsdall and otherwise known by the romantic name of Oleanders.

Schindler's career as an independent domestic architect began with the Schindler-Chase House built in part for his own occupation on Kings Road, Hollywood, in 1921. Here Schindler cast eight-by-four-foot panels of reinforced concrete on the ground and then lifted them into position. He followed this achievement two years later with his Pueblo Ribera Housing built in La Jolla, California, in the same year. Pueblo Ribera, more than just another housing estate, has perhaps never been sufficiently recognized for what it is, namely, a tightly planned settlement where every square inch of built and open space has been carefully accounted for. If ever there were a paradigmatic suburban housing model, economically constructed and designed for a broad range of users, this is it, with its precisely integrated pattern of clearly defined gardens, garages, and U-shaped courtyard houses.

This low-rise, high-density housing scheme directly preceded a sequence of three equally canonical Schindler houses erected in Los Angeles between 1924 and 1926: the Gibling House, the Howe

14

House, and the house on Newport Beach for Dr. Philip Lovell, finished in 1926. Constantly pushing the limits of construction technology, particularly as applied to domestic building, Schindler predicated his Lovell Beach House on five gigantic, in-situ reinforced-concrete frames, within which he deftly suspended a light timber skeleton. Schindler shared this passion for technological innovation with his compatriot Neutra and also with the American Irving Gill, whose pioneering invention of tilt-up slab construction was adopted by Schindler in building his own house. By 1915 Gill had become so proficient in large-scale concrete casting that he succeeded in casting a tilt-up reinforced-concrete wall some sixty feet long and lifting it up as one piece. He later devised all sorts of ingenious treatments for improving the material appearance of concrete, from rubbing color into its surface to painting it with the primary colors mixed with white. His preoccupation with providing hygienic spaces led him to treat the typical wall-to-floor junction with a cast-concrete cove and to install drains in bathrooms and kitchens so that the walls could be easily washed down.

Gill was of the same generation as Wright and had briefly worked with him in the Sullivan and Adler office in Chicago. However, the principles imparted to Gill from Sullivan were quite different from those that Wright followed. Sullivan's interest in African vernacular wall construction encouraged Gill to eliminate all superfluous detail and to strive for an "architecture degree zero," much as Adolf Loos had done in Austria a few years before. Using in-situ concrete walls with large pierced openings as the primary device to this end, Gill designed a series of extremely bare structures, including the Scripps Institution of Oceanography (1908–1910), the Scripps House (1915), and the Dodge House (1914–1916). As with the work of Greene and Greene, Gill's practice suffered from the popularity of the Spanish colonial style. However, he continued to realize radical works in the postwar era, including the low-cost Horatio West Court (1919) and a kindergarten with full-height glass walls, designed in collaboration with John Siebert and built in Oceanside, California, in 1931.

Four years younger than Schindler, Neutra arrived in Los Angeles by a circuitous route, working briefly for the Swiss landscape architect Gustav Amman in 1919 and then for Erich Mendelsohn in Berlin in 1921. Neutra emigrated to the United States in 1923 where he worked briefly for Holabird and Roche in Chicago and then went on to Taliesin in 1924 to work with Wright. In 1925 Neutra moved to Los Angeles and began to collaborate with Schindler, at first only in landscape design. Neutra's independent practice began in 1927 with the commission for the Lovell family home in Los Angeles, received, it would seem, after Schindler had quarreled with Lovell. With a concrete podium and swimming pool and a modular, light steel framework supporting the intermediate floors and the roof, the Lovell Health House was a tour de force in prefabricated construction. Its enthusiastic reception established Neutra's reputation overnight and led, after a brief interval, to a series of commissions that kept him occupied throughout the 1930s. While Schindler continued to work throughout the same period, he seems to have peaked as a designer with his brilliantly stepped vacation house built on Catalina Island in 1928.

H. H. RICHARDSON
GLESSNER HOUSE, 1885–1887

CHICAGO, ILLINOIS

Virtually complete at the time of his death in 1886 at the age of forty-eight, this was the last house that Henry Hobson Richardson would design in his brief career. Its richly detailed interior, modeled after Richardson's masterly Paine House at Waltham, Massachusetts, is sufficient to make this the finest townhouse of his prodigious production, particularly when one recognizes the exceptionally radical nature of its exterior. In this regard we should note that the extreme contrast between the street and the garden facades derived primarily from Richardson's desire to open the primary rooms of the house to a sunlit court situated to the south. To this end, the four-square house of load-bearing masonry overlooked a garden shielded from the street by a cyclopean walling with sparse fenestration—a relative opacity that was particularly emphasized on the Eighteenth Street facade, which

18

only had vertical slits apart from a recessed, semicircular service entrance of monumental proportions. The resulting two-story re-entrant street frontage in roughly dressed but precisely coursed ashlar was so intimidating as to prompt Montgomery Schuyler to write:

The merits of the building as a building, however, are much effaced when it is considered as a dwelling, and the structure ceases to be defensible, except, indeed, in a military sense. The whole aspect of the exterior is gloomy and forbidding and unhomelike, that but for its neighborhood one would infer its purpose to be not domestic, but penal.

The coursed ashlar of the defensive exterior seems to have been inspired by the banded stonework of the Manoir d'Ango in Varengeville, Normandy (1533–1545), which had not only been photographed by Richardson when he was in France, but which had also been subsequently drawn by A. Q. Longfellow Jr., who was Richardson's assistant on the Glessner House commission and would, in effect, add a number of finishing touches to the house after Richardson's death. The Glessners were exceptionally cultivated clients as one may judge from J. J. Glessner's *The Story of a House*, to which we will return. Glessner, an aficionado of architecture, maintained that the stair hall had been derived from the staircase in the Vassall-Craigie Longfellow House

20

in Cambridge, with Longfellow Jr. having introduced the Glessners to the house of his literary uncle. The Glessners were such fastidious clients as to decide in favor of quarry-faced ashlar for the street facades rather than the marble that Richardson preferred, thereby adhering to the sixteenth-century Varengeville model that they admired as much as Richardson and Longfellow. At the same time, the plan of the house was derived, according to Thomas Hubka, from Abingdon Abbey in England, a photograph of which hung in the Glessners' earlier house when Richardson first met them. This sophisticated, medievalizing taste is most evident in the turreted brickwork and quarried ashlar lintels, framing the windows on the garden front, which may be ironically seen, in retrospect, as brutalism *avant la lettre*.

Like the MacVeagh House, the Glessner residence has half-timbered ceilings in all the major ground-floor spaces with coffered paneling in the stair hall, which today is not only graced by the original egg and dart surround of the wood and marble fireplace but also by a com-memorative portrait of the ample Richardson painted shortly before his death. Everything about the interior of this house displays the same progressive, comfortable, but also traditional taste that we find inflected according to the appointment of the room; thus, the horizontally

proportioned coffered paneling in the dining room with its proto–Art Nouveau fireplace surround in blue and white tiles versus the olive green walls above the bookcases in the library, accompanied by a brick chimney breast and brass surrounds. It is typical of Richardson's exoticism that the tiles surrounding the dining room fireplace were DeMorgan replicas of an ancient Persian design. The kitchen, lined with hygienic white-glazed bricks, has a proto-modern character, appropriate to its double-fronted, iron stove, copper extracting hood, and checkerboard-tiled floor. As the director of a major agricultural machinery company, J. J. Glessner was a technocrat in every sense and yet in his memoir, *The Story of a House*, addressed to his children, he wrote:

We slept in this house for the first time on the night of December 1, 1887, and never in the old house after that. The fire on the hearth typified the home, so we carried the living fire from the hearthstone in the old home at Washington and Morgan streets, and with

that started the fire on the new hearth, accompanied by a little ceremony that I don't know if you remember or not; but the old home had been pleasant with many intimate social gatherings—for your mother had ever the genius for generous friendships and hospitality, and the life in the new home must be a continuation of the life so happily lived in the old, and carry on without break its customs and traditions. And so it was with the fire: the old did not go out, the new merely continued its warmth and glow.

After this testament as to what was once the literal tradition of house-warming we may recognize in passing the hypersensitive eclecticism by which Richardson was able to synthesize a vital style through a particularly subtle re-working of the Romanesque, combined with tropes drawn as much from Japan and the Middle East as from Europe. He created an architectural culture appropriate to an ascendant, modernizing, post–Civil War America, one that would transcend the enervating battle of styles that preoccupied much of the European scene.

24

GREENE AND GREENE
GAMBLE HOUSE, 1908

PASADENA, CALIFORNIA

By the turn of the century, Southern California was already the focus of the American dream some two decades before the advent of Hollywood. Within this still semiarid landscape stood the oasis of Pasadena, which briefly provided the idyllic setting for the development of the Greene brothers' bungalow style. This first emerged, in primitive form, in a house that the Greenes built for Arturo Bandini on San Pasqual Street in 1903.

Bandini, of Spanish extraction, had asked them to design a single-story colonial courtyard house with an open veranda on three sides of the court. Inspired by *Ladies Home Journal* and by Gustav Stickley's magazine, *The Craftsman*, the Greenes detailed the Bandini House in the spirit of the American arts and crafts movement, departing from the adobe mission style that the client had initially requested: hence the deep overhanging eaves; the low-pitched, shingle-tiled roofs; and the rubble stone chimney and generous hearth that fully justified the name that Bandini gave to the house—El Hogar.

Even more crucial to the evolution of the style was the Greene brothers' freestanding pergola-cum-portal on the streetfront, which thereafter embodied the syntactical essence of their bungalow manner. By 1903 they were subject to the influence of Japanese

timber construction, as is evident in the pergola that they added to the terrace of the otherwise traditional Culbertson House of 1902.

Exposed to Asian culture through John C. Bentz, a well-established West Coast dealer in Oriental antiques, the Greene brothers strove to create a unique synthesis out of the Stickley crafts movement and the Japanese timber tradition. Hitting their stride with the Sanborn

House in Pasadena of 1903, the Greenes built some thirty residences in Pasadena in the same synthetic style before they attained the apotheosis of their hybrid manner in the Blacker House built on Hillcrest Avenue in 1907 and in the Gamble House erected on Westmoreland Place the following year.

In David Gamble, second-generation heir to the Procter and Gamble soap empire, the Greenes found an ideal client who worked with them closely, from the selection of the site to the addition of an attic that, with the client's consent, was included largely for compositional reasons. The site itself had many desirable natural features, including a view over the Arroyo Seco Canyon toward the San Gabriel Mountains and two fully grown eucalyptus trees. Today two things immediately strike one on encountering the house: first the way in which it rises out of a site that has been groomed to perfection, including a perfectly paved, red-brick driveway that gently sweeps across a lawn to the front porch, and, second, the exceptional generosity of the open plan on the ground floor where the exposed mahogany framing that runs throughout the space greatly contributes to the sense of ease.

As in the Blacker House, heavy beams support large overhangs, and where these are exposed within they are rounded, tapered, pegged, and hand-rubbed to blend in with the equally harmonious timberwork in the rest of the interior, including the trussed beam over the inglenook in the living room and the stepped balustrade to the main stair rising out of the entry hall. A principal feature enriching the latter is the stained and leaded glass that, along with the lighting, was designed by Charles Greene. Instead of the usual leaded joints, the Greene brothers, in conjunction with the Judson Studio, developed their own method for assembling the glass fragments. The strongest exterior is the northeastern facade with its large, open-air sleeping terraces under equally generous, over-sailing timber roofs: a veritable symphony of purlins, rafters, balustrades, rails, brackets, and spigots of various shapes and sizes.

Deliberately eschewing the typical stuffy Victorian style of the period, the Greene brothers proposed the idea of sleeping outside in this winter residence. This modus vivendi reappeared just over a decade or so later in the two health houses that Rudolph Schindler and Richard Neutra built for Dr. Philip Lovell. However, in the Gamble House not only the sleeping porches but also the open ground floor are arranged to take advantage of the prevailing breeze.

The foundations are of clinker brick that was bent and twisted during firing. The same material was also used for the earthwork terrace and Chinese lily pond on the garden side. In the first sketches the house is set at an angle to the road to catch the full force of the prevailing wind, but eventually it had to be re-aligned because of code restrictions.

The dining and living rooms face west over the back garden and terrace toward the mountains. In the spirit of Japanese construction, the Greenes designed every aspect of the house from the overall structure to lighting and furniture, carpets, picture frames, silverware, and even linens, all of which remain in the house.

Key to the realization of the design were the contractors, the Swedish stair builder Peter Hall and his brother John, a cabinetmaker, who were responsible for the basic fabric of the house inside and out.

 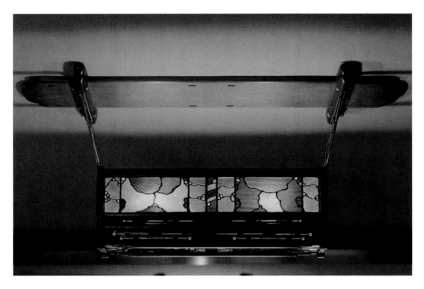

A golden light infiltrates the Gamble House at different times of the day, a feature that no one has captured more convincingly than Reyner Banham, when he wrote in 1977:

Simply you have to be there at all hours . . . to know what the house has to offer . . . to see one stupendous architectural vision that is only available to the early riser around six-thirty of a winter dawn, an hour when even the most assiduous visitor of national monuments is unlikely ever to be in the house. At that hour, on certain favoured mornings, the early prowler will find the sun striking almost horizontally through the upstairs landing from front to back. That in itself is a rewarding sight, but if one then directs one's bare bedroom feet down the warm carpeted stairs to the entrance hall,

one will there find that same low sunlight, already dappled by its passage through the trees across the road opposite, blazing through that fantastic Tiffany glass in the entrance doors and filling the house from front to back with a luminance not to be found anywhere else. It is true that one may find it in small samples in Tiffany lamps, but they only serve as highlights, as Gustav Stickley said, among the mellow radiance of wood tones, while in that entrance hall at sun-up the wood itself is bathed in Tiffany tones from the broad swathes of gold and greenish light that pour through those doors and fall directly upon the paneling or are reflected on it from the floor. That rather formal central space of the house is transformed, for maybe an hour, into something so perfectly "cliché"—Aladdin's cave or a sacred grove—that you know it must be a great work of art because it is so obviously right and complete.

The Gamble House was the closest that American architects would come to the cult of the art nouveau that had been all the rage in Europe throughout the previous decade. Not even Frank Lloyd Wright could equal the sensuous organicism of the Greenes' Tiffany-inspired interiors. This triumph was relatively short-lived, however, for the Greene brothers' practice was effectively cut short by the fashion for the Spanish colonial manner that came in with the Pan Pacific exhibition in San Diego in 1915.

RUDOLPH SCHINDLER
SCHINDLER-CHASE HOUSE, 1921–1922
WEST HOLLYWOOD, CALIFORNIA

Built almost opposite Irving Gill's Dodge House of 1916, Schindler's first work established his reputation on two levels, demonstrating his already proven capacity as a hands-on builder (he and his client, Clyde Chase, built much of the fabric themselves), and his ability to invent a new, liberating space that was far more radical, programmatically speaking, than anything he had pursued while working for Frank Lloyd Wright. First and foremost the Kings Road house was an experiment in communal, cooperative living that stressed to an equal degree the sovereignty of the individual and the concept of sharing. Thus, while the communal kitchen was designed to be shared by two young couples (Schindler and his wife, Pauline Gibling, and Clyde Chase and his wife), each individual had his or her own self-contained studio space in which to retire and even to live somewhat independently from others.

Schindler's own account of the complex, published in *T-Square* in 1932, explains this intention with nuanced directness:

The ordinary residential arrangement providing rooms for specialized purposes has been abandoned. Instead each person receives a large private studio; each couple, a common entrance hall and bath. Open porches on the roof are used for sleeping. An enclosed patio for each couple, with an out-of-door fireplace, serves the purposes of an ordinary living room. The form of the house divides the garden into several such private rooms. A separate guest apartment, with its own garden, is also provided for. One kitchen is planned for both couples. The wives take alternate weekly responsibility for dinner menus, and so gain periods of respite from the incessant household rhythm.

Structurally, the house was largely predicated on a lift-up wall system, in reinforced concrete, pioneered a decade earlier by Irving Gill. Each four-foot-wide precast wall panel was hoisted into its final vertical position by two men using a tripod and a block and tackle. These slabs were graduated in thickness from top to bottom to save material while the standard three-inch gaps between one wall slab and the next were either left open for ventilation or filled with glass. Schindler saw such a wall as having all of the advantages of traditional masonry construction without being heavy and spatially impervious.

Aside from these enclosing walls, which wrap the perimeter of the site to form an introspective courtyard house, the enclosing membrane, comprising sliding side walls, clerestory roof lights, and the built-up roof itself, is of redwood, beautifully worked to produce absolutely minimal sections by Schindler, Chase, and their carpenters. The house's gossamer "filigree in wood" imparts a particular spatiality and charm to Schindler's domestic architecture, and this, together with the ivy running along the pergolas and fascia, gives the whole a lightweight, woven feeling that surpasses in airiness and mobility anything previously achieved by Wright.

Schindler also effectively organized and articulated the site as a landscape, not only in terms of the patio dedicated to each couple but also with regard to subtle changes in level introduced into an otherwise flat domain. Each patio was accompanied by its own sunken garden, a device that, in combination with perimeter hedges, increased the apparent spaciousness of the site.

Not a single square inch was left unaccounted for in Schindler's site plan, and the Japanese atmosphere stemmed from the way in which both the guest suite and the garage contribute to the proliferation of bounded micro-spaces throughout.

Finally, the furniture, as in Wright's work, is largely built-in. Schindler had a particular penchant for L-shaped, continuous seating luxuriously equipped with cushions, which he seems to have pioneered quite a while before Wright used a similar device in his Usonian houses of the 1930s. Schindler's famous wood-framed, "slung" armchair with its suspended canvas seat also appears for the first time in this house.

FRANK LLOYD WRIGHT STORER HOUSE, 1923

HOLLYWOOD, CALIFORNIA

The John Storer House is one of four textile-block houses that Wright designed and executed in the Los Angeles area, the others being the Millard, Freeman, and Ennis houses, all built at virtually the same time. All of these residences stand today, but the Storer House is unique in the exceptional care with which it has been restored to its original condition by the present owner.

Wright developed the so-called textile-block system in an effort to construct houses that would be affordable for the broad American middle class. Concrete block had long since been developed as a cheap method of construction, yet aesthetically it left much to be desired. Wright realized that special molds could redeem this humble material by incorporating a shallow relief pattern into the face of the block. Double-layered, stack-bonded, cavity-wall construction enabled the blocks to be bonded together with reinforcing steel set both vertically and horizontally into pre-formed grooves within the thickness of the block. This weaving of the reinforcement in both directions inspired Wright's term textile block.

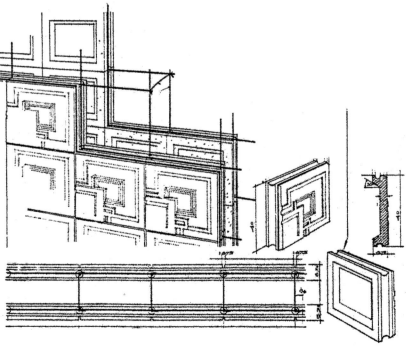

The weaving effect was emphasized by the implicitly spatial character of the blocks themselves since they could be fully perforated and/or filled with glass. With such devices, masonry walls could be partially dematerialized in an unprecedented way, helping Wright to overcome, in an extremely subtle manner, the conventional separation of the interior from the exterior. Above all, the perforations were capable of generating infinite variations in the quality of light and shade. As Wright put it:

... this interior conception took architecture entirely away from sculpture, away from painting and entirely away from architecture as it had been known in the antique. The building now became a creation of interior space in light. And as this sense of the interior space as the reality of the building began to work, walls as walls fell away.

The Storer House stands in the Hollywood Hills overlooking Los Angeles. One approaches it from the street below, with the house terracing back into the hill so as to produce a set of lateral terraces built of the same block as the house. A monumental stairway to one side leads to the main body of the house at the elevated living-room level. The southern orientation of this space allows an optimum amount of sunlight to penetrate into an otherwise quiet and softly lit interior. The front door opens directly into the dining area, with the main stair accessing the second floor located at the other end of the space. A secondary entrance provides direct access from the garage to the kitchen.

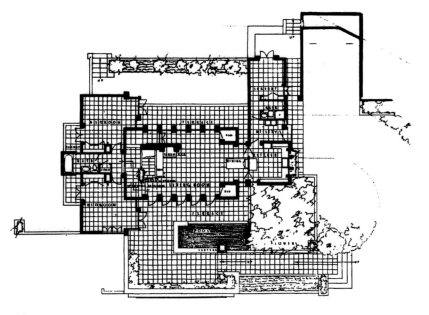

The bedrooms are located on split levels above and below the main space. The main volume, accommodating both dining and living, receives light from both sides via slender windows set between concrete-block piers.

While textile blocks, fair-faced inside and out, constitute the main bearing elements, exposed wooden beams support the floors. The ever-changing light produced by the blocks and the patterning of the blocks themselves eliminate any need for applied decoration. These rich internal effects are complemented by artificial lighting integrated into the walls and ceilings.

The same strategy is also applied on the exterior, particularly in the spotlighting of the podium and its balustrade, which creates an unusually rich effect at night. The whole produces the exotic Oriental effect that Wright seems to have assiduously sought throughout much of his life.

RUDOLPH
SCHINDLER

LOVELL
BEACH HOUSE,
1925–1926

NEWPORT BEACH,
CALIFORNIA

Schindler followed the tour de force of his Hollywood house with two equally canonical achievements, his Pueblo Ribera cottage colony built in San Diego in 1924, and a vacation home, the third and last house that he would design for Dr. Philip Lovell. Schindler exploited each commission as an occasion to experiment with a new method of construction. In this instance, the invention involved raising the house on five in-situ reinforced-concrete cantilever frames, cast in the form of a figure eight, with transverse beams running across the section. These frames are spanned by timber rafters with boarded floors while built-up plaster walls two inches thick are suspended by steel cables from the upper superstructure. Schindler opted for such an expensive and time-consuming structure for three reasons: to maintain a panoramic view over the ocean by elevating the main floor of the

house higher than the adjacent buildings; to provide a covered play area beneath the house; and, finally, to afford an antiseismic superstructure for the entire assembly. Within five years this superstructure proved its worth in an earthquake that destroyed a nearby school while leaving the beach house untouched.

The house consists of two elevated floors: a double-height living room with bedrooms and sleeping decks suspended on a gallery above. A stair and a stepped ramp, both executed in in-situ concrete, afford access to the "servant" and "served" parts of the house with the former rising to the kitchen and maid's quarters on the landward side and the latter providing a more gentle approach to the main living level overlooking the ocean.

50

As in his Kings Road house, Schindler used a horizontal and vertical module to form intervals of four, six, and eight feet as a means of modulating the abstract fenestration as it wove in and out of his concrete superstructure.

This filigree fretwork, of Wrightian origin, gave a particular inflection and rhythm to the house, particularly in conjunction with its built-in furniture, which together with the lighting baffles that occupied the upper part of the living volume gave the house a neo-Plastic look. It is perhaps this exoticism that led to the exclusion of Schindler's work from the Museum of Modern Art's International Style exhibition of 1932.

A salient feature of this house, which invites comparison to the Rietveld/Schroeder House of 1924, is the way in which Schindler attempted to transform its frontal organization into a counterbalancing rotational movement, particularly evident in the way in which viewing balconies turn toward the ocean at the first and second floors.

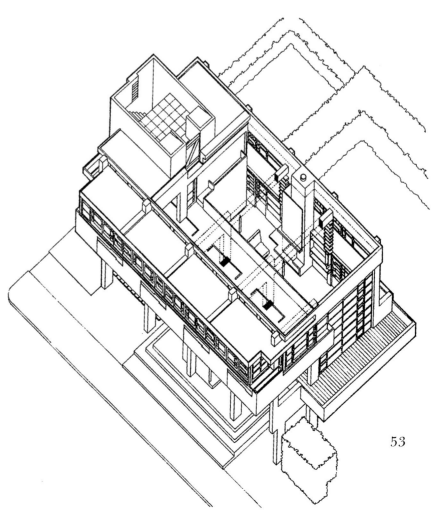

53

With a beach garden below (designed by Schindler's compatriot, Richard Neutra) this house embodies the calisthenic lifestyle favored by Lovell and Schindler alike. At this stage in their careers they were complementary aspects of the same personality, as we may judge from the series of essays that Schindler contributed in the spring of 1926 to Lovell's "Care of the Body" section in the *Los Angeles Times*. These essays afforded Schindler a platform to articulate in words what he had already demonstrated at Newport Beach in three dimensions. This was most cogently stated in the last article of the series, where he commented critically on the use of artificial lighting:

No room should ever be cursed by the provision of an outlet in the center of the ceiling. The use of plugs and movable lamps should be encouraged whenever possible. The popular pair of brackets on either side of the mantel is to be condemned. Anybody sitting in front of a fire will be distressed by their light and will require instead a reading lamp over his shoulder. . . . Anybody lying in bed will prefer a low placed light rather than the glare of a fixture or a lighted ceiling. In general the bulbs require transparent (translucent) shades to distribute and soften the light. In the dining room, however, some exposed direct rays will increase the sparkle of the silver and the lucidity of the glass.

It is just such hypersensitivity to the overall impact of the environment that would be Schindler's legacy to the Southern Californian tradition in twentieth-century architecture.

54

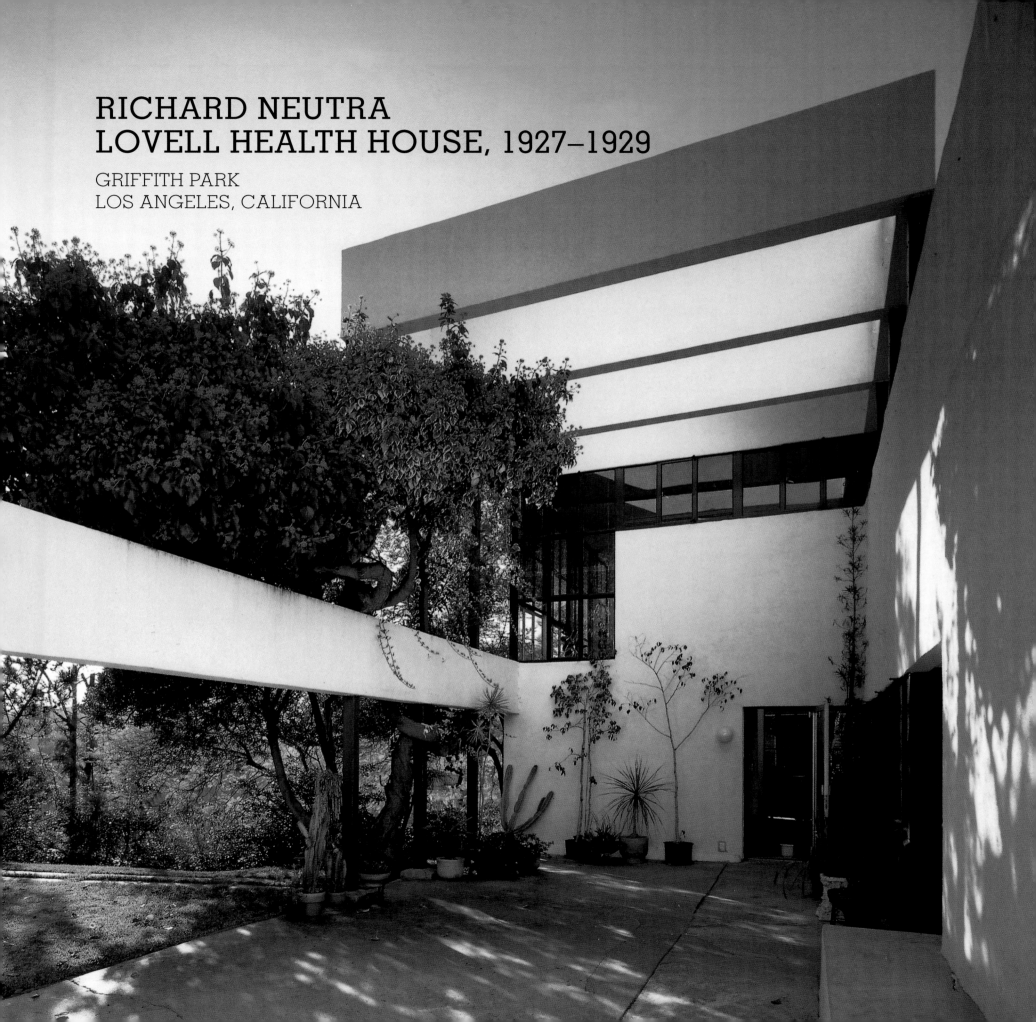

RICHARD NEUTRA
LOVELL HEALTH HOUSE, 1927–1929

GRIFFITH PARK
LOS ANGELES, CALIFORNIA

If any one building epitomizes the International Style in the United States, it is surely Richard Neutra's canonical Lovell Health House that was to demonstrate the ideal correlation between the modern space-form and a new way of life, which, as far as Lovell and Neutra were concerned, was also destined to be a healthier mode of living.
If Dr. Philip Lovell, as architecture buff and nature therapist, was Neutra's ideal client, then Neutra, with his admiration for the medical profession and his comprehensive biorealist approach, was Lovell's ideal architect. The predictable result of their collaboration was an ideal modern house beautifully situated on an idyllic site, and it would be many years before Neutra would equal the vivacity and grandeur of this achievement.

56

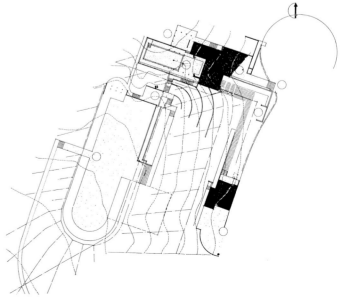

The Health House comprises three separate levels laid into the sides of a steep hill. Apart from a single-story garage, set off to one side, the entry level includes a large stair hall leading down into the main living space, a study, and a series of bedroom suites, each of which has its own sleeping porch.

The second level provides an extremely generous living and dining volume terminating in another sleeping porch at the northwestern end and in a library and patio at the other, opening into the escarpment. Changing its direction, the main stair continues down to a partially covered swimming pool and playroom on the level beneath, which, in turn, has its own independent stair leading out into the site itself. As in all of Neutra's domestic works, the landscape is an essential part of the concept. Here it assumes a wild character as it continues down the rock scree and scrub of the hillside, pausing here and there in a small terrace and retaining wall before terminating at the bottom of the slope in a running track.

At the time it was built, the house was also a technological demonstration comprising a lightweight steel frame of open lattice beams supported on four-inch square tubular columns at five-feet-two-inch centers. This skeleton was clad with metal spandrel panels, standard metal casements, and the occasional solid concrete upstand sprayed onto metal mesh. The only exceptions to this unorthodox hybrid technique were the foundations and the in-situ concrete cross-walls supporting the deadweight of the pool. The open lattice girders enabled Neutra to install the services throughout the house with the greatest ease, while piped cement facilitated the casting of concrete on an otherwise inaccessible site. Last but not least, Neutra achieved certain cantilevers by suspending floor sections from rolled steel joists running transversely across the main frames at the roof level. While the house was intended to demonstrate machine-age production, the finish was uneven since the sprayed concrete was not as smooth as the metal spandrels.

Notwithstanding Neutra's insistence on using the same structural module throughout, the interior of the house is luxuriously and sensitively furnished, almost as though it were a small public institution rather than a private house. Before the conversion of one of the sleeping porches into a dining room, the double-height stair hall with its asymmetrical hearth and continuous L-shaped seating served as the principal living space with the formal dining being set off in one direction and the floor dropping down two steps toward the library in the other. A suspended and inverted light trough in chromium steel runs the entire length of the living and library volumes, unifying the entire space. High-gloss paint, lacquered wood paneling, leather and velvet upholstery, pale gray carpeting, silver-painted metalwork, full-height drapes across all the windows, and plywood sprung-cantilevered chairs of Neutra's own design give the space an austere but exotic feeling, the apotheosis of which was the Ford automobile headlight that was set into the freestanding stair wall, close to the core of the house.

Among the more pragmatic modernizing inventions, the house boasted a fourteen-foot-long patent sink and draining board in the kitchen that had been installed as one piece, complete with vegetable washer, gas-fired incinerator, and water softener.

60

ELIEL SAARINEN
SAARINEN HOUSE

CRANBROOK ACADEMY
OF ART, 1928–1929

BLOOMFIELD HILLS, MICHIGAN

In 1924 Finnish architect Eliel Saarinen was commissioned by George Booth to design a master plan for two high schools and an academy of art to be built on his large estate in Bloomfield Hills, close to Detroit. The client wanted the entire complex to be a self-sufficient microcosm complete with schools and residential accommodation for the faculty and staff. For the next twenty years Saarinen was continuously engaged in realizing the Cranbrook School for Boys, the Kingswood School for Girls, the Institute of Science, plus an art museum, a library, faculty housing, and artists' studios.

This comprehensive project extended to the design of Saarinen's own residence after he assumed directorship of the Academy. This collaborative family effort involved the architect, his wife, Loja, and their children, Eero and Eva-Lisa. Loja Saarinen ran the weaving department at Cranbrook, which enabled her to design and weave rugs, draperies, and textiles for the house. Eero helped design and build the furniture, while Eva-Lisa handled wall and ceiling treatments. In this way the house expressed not only the creative capacity of the family but also the ideology of the academy as a whole.

Today the house is part of a residential street that leads from one of the main entrances into the academy. Built of load-bearing brickwork, it is totally integrated into the terrace of houses of which it forms a part. As in all of the other houses, the front yard is elevated above the sidewalk about four feet while a slightly protruding double-height, gabled facade, with its soldier-course lintels, wood frames, leaded lights, and decorative brickwork, announces its status.

The U-shaped plan of the house is organized about a series of longitudinal and transverse axes. The entry gives directly onto the living room with a framed view of the courtyard beyond. The living room, dining room, pantry, and kitchen are arranged as an enfilade along the transverse axis. One of the courtyard wings accommodates the studio in which Saarinen conducted his classes, while the other houses a covered porch.

The geometric patterns woven into the textiles used throughout the house reflect the building's orthogonal format while the well-crafted furniture is invariably enriched with precious inlaid wood.

Saarinen paid special attention to the design of the light fixtures, particularly to the sconces that provide indirect light to the space. The large fireplace surround in the living room is faced with brown tiles made by Mary Chase Statton in Detroit's Pewabic Pottery. A large silk wall hanging by Loja Saarinen, with a design based on a tree motif, originally hung above the chimney breast in the main space.

The dining room walls are veneered in fir while the circular table inlaid with hollywood was designed by Saarinen. The matching dining chairs inlaid with ebony were made by Tor Berglund of the Cranbrook Studios while the hanging lamp over the center of the table is again by Saarinen.

The bedroom sequence above culminates in the master bedroom suite that, with a fireplace and sitting area, also functions as an adult living space. At one end of this volume is a bay window with built-in seating overlooking the entrance; at the other is the master bathroom elaborately finished in black and tan tiles.

In many respects this house represents a stylistic synthesis of a number of different impulses, ranging from English arts and crafts to Nordic classicism; from Saarinen's own national romantic manner, as we find this in his Finnish career, to the emerging art deco ethos of the late 1920s. A similar range of hybrid stylistic values may be found throughout the Cranbrook campus and in this regard the house was the showpiece of the academy, demonstrating the capacity of the middle-class home to become a total work of art dedicated to a new way of life.

SURVIVAL THROUGH DESIGN:

THE TRIUMPH OF THE MODERN AMERICAN HOUSE, 1929–1945

American modern architecture in the socially liberative sense first emerged in Southern California where the leading pioneers were Irving Gill, Rudolph Schindler, and Richard Neutra. After his initial efforts, the architect who rose to prominence in the 1930s was Neutra, whose remarkable achievements during this decade have yet to be fully acknowledged. In the field of domestic architecture Neutra realized one remarkable work after another beginning with his 1932 VDL Research House (fig. 1), built in the Silver Lake area of Los Angeles. This house, financed by the Dutch industrialist and modern architecture patron C. H. Van der Leeuw, was designed as an experiment and finished in unorthodox materials including enameled metal panels for the facade and cork tile pressed onto fiberboard for the floor. The two-story main block on the streetfront housed Neutra's office and study on the ground floor with the family apartment above, complete with an ample terrace overlooking the lake and the mountains beyond. The patio area to the rear was sensitively landscaped, affording an exotic garden best appreciated through the sliding glass walls of the lower rear apartment.

The single-story Beard House (fig. 2), built in Altadena in 1935, was even more progressive in that its walls were made of standard hollow sheet-metal floor elements. These, in turn, carried lightweight metal trusses supporting a composite flat roof and a hollow floor suspended above the ground slab. Neutra used this hollow construction as a plenum system for the distribution of warm or cool air, depending on the season. Despite the standard prefabricated elements, this house, with its glistening metal skin, was an extremely lyrical work. Intimately connected to the surrounding landscape by deftly placed pergolas and sliding glass walls, the whole was enriched by an elegant, tubular steel stair giving access to a roof deck above. Neutra repeated this "metallic syntax"[1] in one house after another, large and small, throughout the 1930s. These houses were often commissioned by rather eccentric clients such as the psychologist Galka Scheyer and the dance therapist Grace Lewis Miller.[2] At the other extreme were technocrats such as William Beard, who was on the faculty at Cal Tech. The emigré intellectuals of Hollywood also patronized Neutra during the 1930s. It was through these connections that he came to build a remarkable steel house in the San Fernando Valley for Josef von Sternberg in 1936.

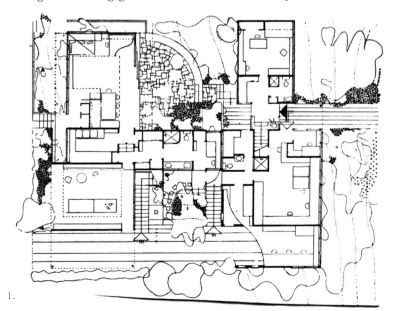

1.

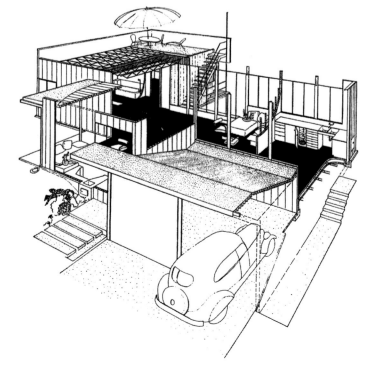

2.

Neutra's 1951 description of the house (fig. 3), after its purchase by the novelist Ayn Rand, gives a vivid account of the various environments that were incorporated into its form:

Pool, tennis courts, garden land and orchards are placed around the building on a plot of twenty acres. The access from the west is accompanied by a row of eucalyptus trees and one enjoys a wonderful view of the mountains in the north and in the south. The walls of the patio are copper bearing steel, aluminum coated. At the end of the patio is a roofed entrance. The living quarters are large and high and extend through two floors. They open onto the patio with its semicircular ending. The patio and living quarters have a floor of black terrazzo. The entire skeleton and the enclosure is of steel. The room at the end of the living quarters is cooled by artificial rain which descends into the patio. The master bedroom opens onto a roof pool for tropical fish. [3]

The approach to the house was conceived as though it were the terminus of an automotive trajectory (recalling that of Le Corbusier's Villa Savoye of 1929). Cars entered and left the compound on precisely delineated concrete tracks laid into the greensward surrounding the house. This entry was reinforced topographically by the provision of an ornamental moat surrounding the ribbed metal stockade of the semicircular patio.

Neutra created an equally technocratic house, with the unintentionally ironic name of Windshield, for a patrician family on Fishers Island in 1938. [4] In addition to copper-coated steel cladding anodized in aluminum, Neutra experimented here with Solex heat-resistant glass. He also installed a prototypical prefabricated, drop-in bathroom unit designed by R. Buckminster Fuller. This was made of silver-antimony-coated copper and equipped with integral fixtures, indirect lighting, and an electrically operated sliding door.

Unlike the works of many other architects who participated in the so-called International Style, Neutra's interiors were sensuously furnished. They were comfortable and luxurious and the main living volumes invariably opened onto sensitively designed, exotic gardens, backed by spectacular landscapes. As one satisfied client wrote in 1937:

When we built the house for my mother, she expected to live in it three months of the year. She shared, by the way, the popular prejudice against modernistic architecture. When she saw the house she did not feel the "istic" quality at all, but looked upon it as a home, and right away planned spending half her time, six months out of each year, in it. But after she began using the convenient work room and bathroom and dressing room, without ever consciously changing her plans, she has accepted this place as her home.

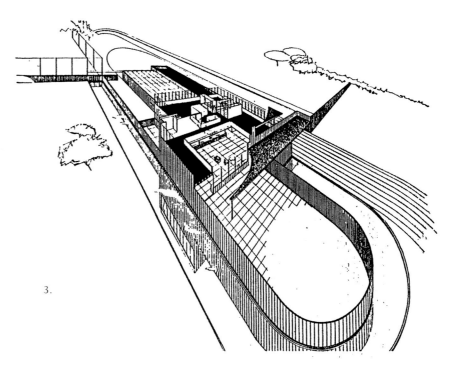

3.

She dislikes very much any trip that takes her away overnight from it, and the longer the vacation away from this house, the more she resents it. [5]

Influenced by Schindler's Pueblo Ribera housing and in general by the bungalow court culture of Southern California, Neutra realized a similar settlement pattern in his Strathmore Apartments of 1938 (fig. 4), built in the Westwood area of Los Angeles and consisting of

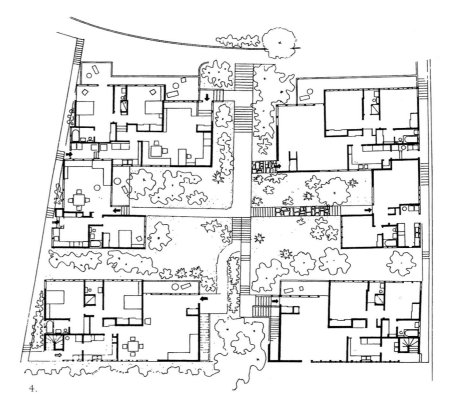

4.

six two-bedroom and four one-bedroom apartments. Planned on a 39½-inch module and faced in standard steel casements, the units are stacked on a sloping site with built-in garages. This subtle terracing was enriched by stepped courtyard gardens that flow from one terrace to the next. The development was initially occupied by members of the Hollywood elite including such figures as Dolores Del Rio, Orson Welles, Luis Rainer, Clifford Odets, and Lilly Latte and her companion, Fritz Lang. In 1950 John Entenza, editor of the influential magazine *Arts and Architecture*, came to live in the Strathmore Apartments, abandoning his own Case Study house because it lacked intimacy. Entenza, in effect, replaced Charles and Ray Eames who had lived in a Strathmore apartment for eight years before moving to their own prefabricated house on the Pacific Palisades in 1949.

Between the McIntosh House of 1937, clad in redwood siding, and the brick house that Neutra built in Brentwood in 1942 for the NBC radio producer John Nesbitt, the architect relinquished his all-metal silver syntax of the 1930s to engage in a more natural expression that is also evident in his masterly Channel Heights Housing in San Pedro, California. Roofed by timber joints spanning onto built-up timber beams, the Nesbitt House (fig. 5) is an unusual mixture of minimalist fenestration with neo-brutalist brickwork.

As the site plan indicates, this house recalls the atmosphere of a traditional Japanese house and garden, without being in the slightest way Japanesque. Neutra was closer at this moment perhaps to Alvar Aalto than to any other contemporary practitioner.

5.

Schindler was as active in the 1930s as Neutra, although he did not receive such prestigious commissions nor did he enjoy the same level of international recognition. This rather inexplicable neglect began with his exclusion from the 1932 Museum of Modern Art International Style exhibition, curated by Henry-Russell Hitchcock and Philip Johnson. However, of the thirty houses that he realized between the Wolfe House built on Catalina Island in 1928 and his death twenty-five years later at the age of sixty-six, few attain the stature of Neutra at his best. Schindler's residences were structurally ingenious, intimate, and sensitive, but, with the singular exception of the Buck House of 1934, they were not decisive stylistically. However, as Henry Plummer has written, the Buck House was a remarkably complex and poetic work:

The crystalline-white Buck House by Rudolph Schindler is a complex form-field made out of offset and loosely intersected planes and corners. As in De Stijl paintings, the negative forms, the immaterial cavities and fissures, are essential if not primary elements in the composition. Absence becomes presence, the intangible figures making their own appearance as shapes of light, or as colored patches of nature and city seen through "windows," the latter now mutating plastic cut-outs rather than stable holes in a wall. The many planes and corners produce an ever-changing mobile fabric whose interlaced sheets keep re-forming as we move, a kinetically charged yet well-ordered balance of broken stereometric fragments. Volumes are rendered slightly incomplete, especially along key defining edges, so that they turn perceptually active in their drives toward closure. Horizontal roof planes leap from one cubic volume into another, then project and overhang, interlocking the freestanding screens, experienced as a shifting and sliding collage, the cut-out layers perpetually appearing and disappearing, separating and overlying. Gaps in material are roughly aligned through successive layers of rooms to multiply the interfering layers, energized by their perceptual drive to be extricated from each other and as fragments the eye struggles to make whole. The file of walls and roofs is onion-like in its half-transparent wrappings, each room seeming to be enveloped by another one just beyond. There is even a faint psychological activity, a residue of the frontier adventure, in these seductively mysterious and beckoning horizons. And while anti-nature in conception, the house provides intense communication with nature through its porous walls, and by interpenetrative masses that have wrapped about and opened to gardens through extensive glass walls.[6]

It should perhaps be noted in passing that Neutra and Schindler, like other Southern Californian intellectuals and artists of their generation, were committed to a socialist agenda and that Pauline Gibling, Schindler's wife, remained a political radical to the end of her life.

In the Midwest the mission of propagating the modern movement in architecture in the 1930s lay mainly with George Fred Keck and his younger brother William Keck. Keck and Keck opened their practice by designing two remarkable exhibition houses that were consecutively featured in Chicago's Century of Progress exhibition, which opened in 1933 (fig. 6), and ran for two years. The first house, the so-called House of Tomorrow of 1933, with its dodecahedron plan, seems to have been derived in part from Orson Fowler's Octagon House of 1848 and in part from Buckminster Fuller's Dymaxion House of 1927.

However, where the central mast of the Dymaxion House contained mechanical services, the core of the House of Tomorrow accommodated a spiral stair that served its three levels. Built on concrete foundations, with fiber-concrete floor slabs, the House of Tomorrow

6.

was made of a cross-braced structural steel frame with shop-fabricated infill panels and slender columns supporting the outer edges of the floors. The interior was extensively furnished in glass panels of various colors while the exterior was initially sheathed in plate glass.

In 1934 Keck and Keck designed their second exhibition house, an orthogonal and more practical version known as the Crystal House (fig. 7). This three-story dwelling was supported by an exoskeleton of lattice trusses directly tied into its reinforced-concrete floors and roof. As in the House of Tomorrow, different types of glass were used for each of the three floors. The planning of the interior was uncannily

Miesian, given the date, and so was the furniture. Keck and Keck made the first recorded use of Mies van der Rohe's patent pieces in the United States, in particular the Tugendhat and MR chairs that appeared here for the first time only a few years after their initial production. Up-to-the-minute in every respect, Keck also installed Buckminster Fuller's prototypical Dymaxion Car in the ground-floor garage.

Their participation in the Century of Progress Exhibition brought Keck and Keck to the attention of a wealthy clientele, and the firm went on to design a wide range of modern residences throughout the next twenty years, including the remarkable Herbert Bruning House in Wilmette, Illinois, and the Cahn Residence in Lake Forest, both dating from 1936. Apart from pioneering the domestic use of glass block, these houses were also the proving ground for many other technical innovations. The Bruning House was of particular importance for its synthesis of modern materials with advanced methods for climate control that included the installation of purpose-made, chain-activated external Venetian blinds. The house was very precisely sited from the point of view of orientation and these concerns would preoccupy the Keck brothers for the rest of their practice. From the mid-1930s the Keck and Keck firm was a pioneer in the field of passive solar energy design.

After the influential Museum of Modern Art exhibition in 1932, modern architecture attained an acceptable social status that enabled it to remain in the ascendant on the East Coast until 1945. Thus the 1930s saw a proliferation of modern architecture on the North American continent, particularly in the field of domestic building.

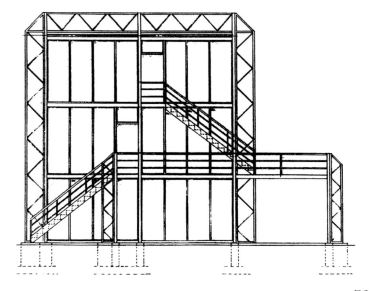

7.

73

Aside from the work of the Keck brothers and Neutra, James and Katherine Morrow Ford's anthology *The Modern House in America* of 1940 featured the early work of the next generation of Southern Californian architects such as Hamilton Harwell Harris, Raphael Soriano, and Gregory Ain, all of whom had served as Neutra's assistants; the early work of the Bauhaus emigré architects, Walter Gropius and Marcel Breuer; the transitional works of more traditional architects such as Phillip Goodwin, George Howe, and Edward Durrell Stone; and, finally, the residential architecture of other emigré modernists such as William Lescaze and Albert Frey. The Swiss emigré Lescaze requires particular mention not only for the Field House that he and Howe realized in New Hartford, Connecticut, in 1932 but also for his own townhouse erected in Manhattan in 1934 (fig. 8) that combined within a typical brownstone an architect's office on the ground floor and a three-story living unit above. The house was distinguished by an all-glass block facade and by a freestanding column carrying a thin concrete canopy over the entrance.

The successors to Neutra and Schindler, whom Esther McCoy identified as the second generation of the California school in her book of 1984, were all active on their own by 1935. Ain had three or four houses underway by that time. Harris, after initially following Neutra, turned back to the syntax of Wright and even to that of Greene and Greene over the next decade, while Soriano, the most faithful follower of Neutra's stressed-skin manner, finally broke through to his own method of using widely spaced steel frames in his prefabricated houses of the 1940s. As McCoy points out:

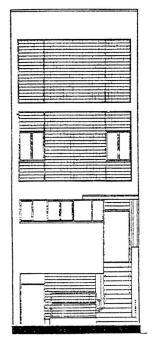

8.

By 1949 he had abandoned the Neutra module (as had Neutra) and used glass in the largest available sheet the budget would bear. He had begun to use steel framing after the war as soon as the restrictions allowed, setting pipe columns at the edge of the overhang, which created a gallery around the house.[7]

The odd man out in this generation was the German emigré J. R. Davidson who in fact arrived in the United States at the same time as Neutra. Working on interiors and small shops for over a decade, Davidson finally came into his own as a residential architect with an elegant house built in Santa Monica in 1937 for Herbert Stothart, the music director of MGM studios. Of the principles behind his sensitive domestic planning Davidson wrote:

For a house I want to achieve serenity and cheerfulness. Most people value these in a house but few clients understand the plan features which produce them. Serenity is achieved through order. The continuous line is a restful one. I line up the cabinets and storage spaces in the living room. I make it a design habit that nothing hangs free of the continuous line except for an accent. The success of the living room does not depend upon size. It is more important that they have both a major and minor axis. They must have both light and shadow—that is why I use light on two sides of a room only.[8]

The so-called New Empiricism that emerged in Europe and on the East Coast after World War II had its origins, as far as America was concerned, in the practice of Walter Gropius and Marcel Breuer, above all in the houses that they designed for themselves and for James and Kathleen Morrow Ford in Lincoln, Massachusetts, and in the vacation house built on the beach at Cohasset for Josephine Haggerty in 1938. Breuer's penchant for mixing local rubble-stone walling with clapboarded balloon-frame construction, painted white, and occasionally relieved by tongue and grooved boarding in natural timber, established the essential syntax of his regionally inflected Bauhaus manner. This appeared in one house after another, attaining perhaps its most elegant expression in the Chamberlain Cottage built in Wayland, Massachusetts, in 1940.

After the war, Breuer went on alone to become one of the country's most prolific architects working at the domestic scale, building extensively on the East Coast and elsewhere and exercising a strong influence on the work of the students at the Graduate School of Design at Harvard; in particular one might note on the residential architecture of Edward Larrabee Barnes. While Breuer's houses were invariably practical, inventive, and comfortable, they were often rather unresolved in formal terms. The striking exception to this was the timber-clad house that he built for himself in New Canaan, Connecticut, in 1945.

Although Frank Lloyd Wright was deliberately excluded from the Ford anthology, no summary of this period can be complete without acknowledging the importance of the Usonian house. The principles were first formulated with the Malcolm Wiley House, built outside Minneapolis in 1932. While a great deal of Wright's domestic work in the 1930s may be loosely classified as Usonian, including the spectacular Fallingwater designed for Edgar Kaufmann in Bear Run, Pennsylvania, in 1936, the Usonian principles were first completely elaborated in the Herbert Jacobs House (fig. 9) in Madison, Wisconsin, of the same year. Wright's solution to the problem of the small house was to divide the accommodation required into living and sleeping wings and to bring these together at right angles at the point of entry. This last also housed a service core made up of the kitchen, the bathroom, and a boiler plus main chimney stack. Wherever it was appropriate Wright turned the windowless rear of the typical Usonian house to the street and opened up the interior to the garden. In this way he simultaneously ensured the privacy of the garden while liberating the interior to its maximum capacity. Structuring this L-shaped plan on a four-foot by two-foot module, Wright took advantage of standard mill sizes and facilitated the prefabrication and installation of all components. In this remarkably accessible and human synthesis, he brought the Prairie Style up-to-date and made it available to the average middle-class family, not only in terms of cost but also from the point of view of cultural accessibility.

Wright designed and realized some two hundred variations of this Usonian prototype during the last thirty years of his life, ranging from the hexagonal Usonian to the so-called Usonian Automatics that rationalized his earlier adoption of textile concrete block construction. The critical success of the Usonian house resides in its suitability and relevance to megalopolitan regional development. It is sobering to realize that this was perhaps the last serious attempt made by any American architect to render the suburb as a place of cultivation. From this point of view, the attributes of the standard L-shaped Usonian house deserve to be itemized. They are: (1) the provision of a clearly defined, private garden enclosed on two sides by the sleeping and living wings; (2) the suppression of the dining room and the opening up of the interior through a series of full-height doors facing south onto a garden terrace; (3) the economical consolidation of all the services at one point; (4) the provision of radiant heating throughout via hot water pipes cast permanently into the ground slab—this same system being used for cooling in summer by circulating cold water in the pipes; (5) the standardization of all horizontal dimensions

according to a four-by-two-foot grid and all vertical dimensions according to a one-foot-one-inch module; (6) the finishing of the entire house in fair-faced natural materials, brick and timber, eliminating the need for plaster (the concrete floor is dyed red and thereafter waxed and kept polished); (7) the treatment of all access corridors as long rooms, lined with storage walls; similar storage walls isolate one bedroom from the next; (8) the use of clerestories throughout to provide backlighting and ventilation and as a device to bring down the apparent height of the house; (9) the provision of roof overhangs throughout for sun shading and for the protection of the walls from rain without metal down pipes; and, finally, (10) the full integration of the house with the surrounding topography.

One should note that the Alan IW Frank House was inserted in this section of the book not only because of the outstanding quality of this oddly neglected work but also because it is one more attempt on our part at adequately representing the American career of Marcel Breuer from the standpoint of domestic building. While we are aware of numerous other Breuer houses that might have been included, we nonetheless felt that his exceptional capacity as a mid-century designer of richly articulated interiors could hardly be better represented than through the Frank House. Although this house is equally credited to Gropius it is fairly clear that the furnishing of the interior was, to all intents and purposes, exclusively the work of Breuer.

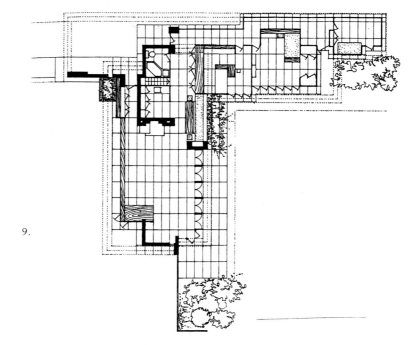

9.

CEDRIC GIBBONS
DOLORES DEL RIO
HOUSE, 1931

SANTA MONICA, CALIFORNIA

Designed by Cedric Gibbons, the art director of MGM from 1924 to 1956, this brilliant work was ostensibly shaped to meet the taste of his wife, actress Dolores del Rio. Coming from a family of architects, Gibbons had studied architecture and was briefly apprenticed to his father before entering set design and moving to Los Angeles in 1918, where he became involved with the fledgling film industry. While Gibbons built very little, he nonetheless exercised considerable influence on the American public, who, regularly exposed to the fictitious interiors that he designed for MGM, began to acquire a liking for modern architecture. Gibbons, for his part, thought of himself as a leading modern architect. This assessment was confirmed, at least locally, by his inclusion in an exhibition otherwise dedicated to the works of Richard Neutra and Rudolph Schindler. As Donald Albrecht has written:

With a propaganda outlet that no architect could ever attain, Gibbons viewed himself not as a slavish imitator of his more exalted brethren but as an equal partner in the promulgation of modern architecture in the United States. . . . [He combined] the glass walls, flexible planning, and asymmetry of the International Style with the robust, cubistic massing of the De Stijl aesthetic.

78

Although Albrecht alludes to the hybrid character of the del Rio House, there is nothing strictly neo-Plastic about its form. Its design, aside from its general air of modernity, has more to do with the art deco movement than with the metaphysical aesthetic of De Stijl.

The front of the house, facing east and virtually windowless, contrasts with the rear, which opens westward toward a view of Santa Monica and the Pacific Palisades, an area that in pre-freeway Los Angeles was sparsely populated. Originally known as West Front, the interior of the house was infused with a sense of luxury, recalling not only Neutra at his best, but also Rob Mallet-Stevens and even Eileen Gray.

The layout is unusual in that the main window of the ground-floor reception room facing the terrace is crossed by a theatrical staircase leading up to the twenty-five-by-forty-five-foot living room with built-in banquettes. Two bedrooms open off this space—one for del Rio and the other for guests. Gibbons's own bedroom, on the ground floor, was equipped with a ladder and a secret trap door that afforded direct access to the del Rio suite above.

This eccentric feature, reminiscent of Madame Dalsace's retractable companion ladder in the Maison de Verre in Paris, has since been removed.

The circulation is accented by stepped reveals over every doorway, a device that seems to anticipate Carlo Scarpa's zig-zag motif of half a century later. Exotic materials are deployed throughout from the facing of the front door in Monel (an alloy of stainless steel and copper then used for aircraft propellers) to the pale green terrazzo finish covering the main stair; from the black linoleum used as flooring to the extensive use of nickel-plated steel, stainless steel, and chromium. The rich material palette goes on to include Bakelite, vitrolite, black terrazzo, and copper sheet that is applied inside and out, from the burnished fireplace surround to the roof covering. To this we must add Gibbons's ingenious use of mirrored walls, particularly in the reception room where they amplify the space beyond the room's already generous proportions and in the living room, above the fireplace, where a horizontal strip reflects the horizon of the Pacific Ocean.

Full-height wall mirrors also line del Rio's bathroom and dressing room and appear again in the dining room, where a mirrored alcove reflects the glazed corner of the room. In both instances they provide the illusion of space beyond. This consistent Wrightian rupturing of the box in its corners extends to the treatment of the west facade, where horizontally profiled steel-sash windows wrap around the corners and flood the interior with natural light.

The general feeling of luxury is reinforced by extensive built-in seating, indirect strip lighting, and flat cylindrical ceiling lights in opaque glass.

Gibbons included such theatrical gestures as glazed lighting panels set into the reverse face of the steps to the main staircase. He also exploited the depth of screen walls and pedestals for the provision of additional storage. These cubistic accents are placed at strategic points in the circulation: at the main entrance and in del Rio's dressing room, where they provide additional table surface as well as storage. Elsewhere they generally serve as pedestals for small works of art.

FRANK LLOYD WRIGHT
FALLINGWATER, 1935–1937

BEAR RUN, PENNSYLVANIA

Designed for Edgar Kaufmann, a Pittsburgh department store owner, in half a day when Wright was sixty-seven years old, Fallingwater is surely Wright's ultimate romantic statement. Unencumbered on this wooded, undulating terrain by the "earth-line" of his mystical midwestern prairie, Wright made the concrete terraces of this house appear as an agglomeration of stacked trays miraculously suspended in space, poised at varying heights in the midst of a forest. Tied back into the rock escarpment, Fallingwater practically defies photography through its all but total fusion with the landscape. Despite the closely spaced horizontal glazing used throughout, nature permeates the structure at every turn. Indeed its interior evokes a furnished cave rather than a house in the conventional sense. That the fieldstone walls and rock-paved floors are intended to pay homage to the site seems to be confirmed by the suspended stairway that drops through a glazed hatchway in the living-room floor to descend to the waterfall below. These stairs have no function other than to bring one into momentary communion with the surface of the running stream.

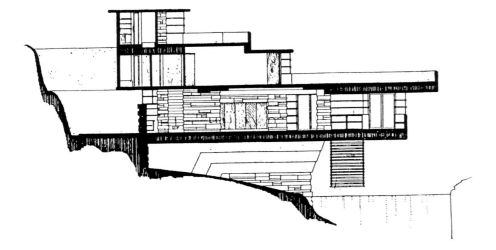

The main house—a relatively modest four-bedroom weekend accommodation poised on two floors above a vast living room with a kitchen, outriding terraces, and a plunge pool attached—was constructed between 1935 and 1937. The so-called guest wing, comprising a four-car garage, two servants' rooms above, and a guest living suite to one side, was erected two years later. Some eighteen feet separate the principal floors of the main house and the guest suite, a difference to be negotiated by a concrete canopied walkway stepping up the slope around a semicircular trajectory.

Wright's perennial drive to juxtapose nature and culture as explicitly as possible took on a particularly dramatic character in the projection of an eighteen-foot, clear-span concrete cantilever over the crest of the waterfall from which it derives its name.

However natural this cantilever may have seemed to Wright, it was almost beyond the capacity of reinforced concrete to perform such a feat, let alone that of the various engineers who calculated and supervised the construction, including William Wesley Peters, Wright's son-in-law, and Mendel Glickman. Thus, despite the twenty-four-inch upstand beams at forty-eight-inch centers set beneath the slab floor and reinforced with one-inch-diameter steel bars, the builders did not allow sufficiently for the deflection of the entire assembly. The barely perceptible sag that developed, together with settlement cracks, were equally disquieting to both client and architect. Wright's engineers regretted their failure to exploit the full structural depth of the upstand balustrade, although it is hard to see how this could have had an appreciable effect on the problem.

The house is furnished with micro-spaces and mythical incidents throughout, from the steps over the stream to the boulder hearth that seems to burst up out of the flagstone floor; from the Jacques Lipchitz sculpture *Mother and Child* added to one side of the plunge pool to the concrete trellis over the driveway behind the house. One of the oddest features of the interior is a spherical metal kettle that swings in and out of position on a welded steel pivot. This curious device had been initially designed for the express purpose of heating wine punch over an open fire. However, Edgar Kaufmann could only recall this device having been used once and even then only after the punch had already been warmed in the kitchen.

90

WALTER GROPIUS
GROPIUS HOUSE, 1937

LINCOLN, MASSACHUSETTS

Of the desirable residential areas that surround Cambridge, few compare to the groomed rusticity of Lincoln. Amid this bucolic landscape Gropius built three houses on the same ample site: one for himself, another for his partner, the ex-Bauhaus master Marcel Breuer, and the third for the housing historian James Ford and his wife, with Breuer presumably playing a key role in the design of all of them. Gropius's own home, as pristine today as when it was completed, owes as much to the cubist forms of the Bauhaus masters' houses that he had designed for Dessau in 1925 as it does to the American tradition of the white clapboarded, balloon-frame dwelling. However, no emigrants were more aware of fundamental transatlantic differences than Walter and Ise Gropius. They saw their migration to the eastern seaboard of the United States as a pioneering experience, and many of the more subtle regional features of the house reflect their awareness of the New England landscape and its climate.

Ever attentive to the moods of the place, Gropius took the advice of his benefactor, the owner of the land, Mrs. James Storrow, when she told him to build his garage away from the house and closer to the main road, in order to reduce the clearing of snow to a minimum. Similar climatic conditions determined the placement of the house on the flat crest of a gentle slope to take full advantage of cooling summer breezes.

Closed on its northern face, save for a strip of windows, the house opens to two paved terraces on its southern side. The larger of these is covered with a flat roof and fully enclosed by screens in order to serve as an outdoor breakfast terrace. There, as elsewhere in the house, roller blinds control the quantity and quality of sunlight.

More sculptural than most photographs suggest, the Gropius House is a dynamic spatial composition that draws one toward the front door, through the passage of an over-sailing canopy, and past an equally compelling wall plane executed in glass block. Beyond the threshold, this inflected movement turns into the unexpected vortex of the stair hall. A continuous black-lacquered handrail that curves effortlessly upward through the double-height space to the second floor emphasizes the sculptural spiral of a dogleg stair. This feature is reinforced by semicircular wall sconces mounted on the walls of white vertically lapped siding that throw indirect light upward.

This four-bedroom house, equipped with four baths, a sewing room, and a study, could hardly have been more economically planned. Nevertheless, the feeling of expansiveness derives from the ingenious use of transitional space throughout so that one rarely encounters a corridor in the true sense. Gropius fully exploited ancillary space so that the first-floor study also serves as an alternative means of access between the entry hall and main living volume. Something similar occurs on the second floor, where access to the master bedroom is through Ise Gropius's dressing room, which also gives onto the main bathroom.

The warmth of this house, reinforced by the cork-tile flooring that runs throughout, distances this work from the more machinist aura of Gropius's Weimar functionalism. A sense of relaxed comfort pervades the interior, despite the freestanding glass-block wall that divides the study from the dining space and the Bauhaus furniture, designed by Marcel Breuer. These Bauhaus elements, which Gropius shipped over during his exodus, are among the dwelling's prominent period pieces. Along with paintings by Laszlo Moholy-Nagy and Alexander Schawsinsky, they bestow a uniquely transatlantic aura— one that recalls the pioneering days of the Museum of Modern Art and

Black Mountain College in North Carolina. This house evokes those halcyon years at Harvard when Joseph Hudnut charged Gropius and other emigré luminaries with the task of totally recasting the curriculum of the Graduate School of Design.

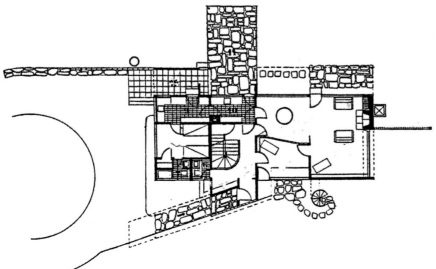
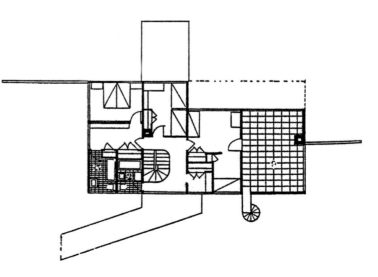

Not without irony, the Gropius House has now become the property
of the Society for the Preservation of New England Antiquities. On
the occasion of its fiftieth anniversary in 1988, the society restored
the house and opened it to the public. In bequeathing it to the society
Ise Gropius intended that the house should not only serve as an
example of Gropius's contribution to modern architecture but also
that its entire contents should provide a reminder of a way of life that
was already becoming remote. To this end Walter Gropius's spectacles
lie on top of his sketch pad and Ise's red evening dress hangs in the
dressing room closet as mutual mute reminders of another time.

WALTER GROPIUS AND MARCEL BREUER ALAN IW FRANK HOUSE, 1939

PITTSBURGH, PENNSYLVANIA

The Frank House in Pittsburgh is the most luxurious residence designed by Walter Gropius and Marcel Breuer. Commissioned by Cecelia and Robert Frank a few years after the architects had both migrated from Europe to the States in the late 1930s, the Frank House appears to be, in retrospect, a unique synthesis of two different approaches—while its overall appearance adhered to the precepts of the International Style of the interwar years, its sumptuous furnishings and its sculptured landscaped setting with fieldstone walling exemplified the ethos of Breuer's so-called New Humanism. This subtly modulated modernity is immediately evident in the interior with its carpeted, freestanding reinforced-concrete staircase that passes through two successive flights in order to provide a spatial link

between the entry, the main living level, and the bedroom floor above. A superstructure on the roof containing storage and services terminates the three-story mass of the house, while the roof itself served in the summer as a roof deck and a dance floor.

The first-floor living level is arranged as a continuous fluid space, which, organized around a central hearth, flows into a series of discreet settings, comprising reception, living, dining, and study areas, as well as an ample terrace situated above the ground-floor swimming pool. This last measures 40 by 20 feet and is directly accessible from the upper part of the site and from the garden level below via a sculptural freestanding stair made of in situ concrete.

The radial seating of the main living volume, focused on a generous hearth built into a travertine stone wall, has a markedly amphitheatrical character. The adjacent dining space, with its expandable dining table, may be readily separated from the adjacent children's dining area through a sliding-folding screen. The six-person table for everyday use may be readily extended so as to seat twenty-four. The bedroom floor above the living level is treated as a self-contained family unit that, in addition to accommodating six bedrooms with en suite bathrooms, also includes a family living room (pictured here) with its own fireplace and a deck situated over the entry lobby at grade.

The luxurious atmosphere of the interior derives in large measure from the provision of thick carpeting throughout and from the combination of venetian blinds with shantung silk curtains. The other elements giving the house its unique character are the upholstered, cantilevered, cut-out laminated plywood chairs such as Breuer had first pioneered in the bent plywood pieces that he had designed for Jack Pritchard in London in the mid-1930s.

The light color of the exposed and sealed plywood paneling and furniture was generally offset by the darker brown and red fabric used

100

for the upholstery. Breuer occasionally highlighted this palette with zebra-hide cushions. The upper floors were extensively equipped with built-in desks, tables, and bookshelves, made of either redwood or maple plywoods. A variety of wall coverings were used, ranging from travertine to a woven copper material designed by Anni Albers and textured wallpaper featuring an American Indian theme in the guest room. Some 160 pieces of bespoke furniture were specifically made for the house along with innumerable lighting units, most of them being built-in or totally concealed. The perimeter heating was encased in skirting boards perforated with circular holes. Other wall surfaces were lined with pearwood and English sycamore.

Except for the tubular steel balustrading filled with copper-covered steel mesh, the occasional glass block floor or wall, and the full-height plate-glass windows of the ground floor, there was little here that derived from the Bauhaus aesthetic, as we find this, say, in Breuer's chromium-plated tubular steel Wassily Chair of 1927 or in Gropius's houses for the Bauhaus of the same date. The delicate rhythm of the welded steel frame, with its exposed stanchions recessed into the salmon-colored kasota-stone cladding, divides the rectangular mass of the house into six bays, which, together with the horizontal windows spanning from stanchion to stanchion, provide for a harmoniously proportioned composition.

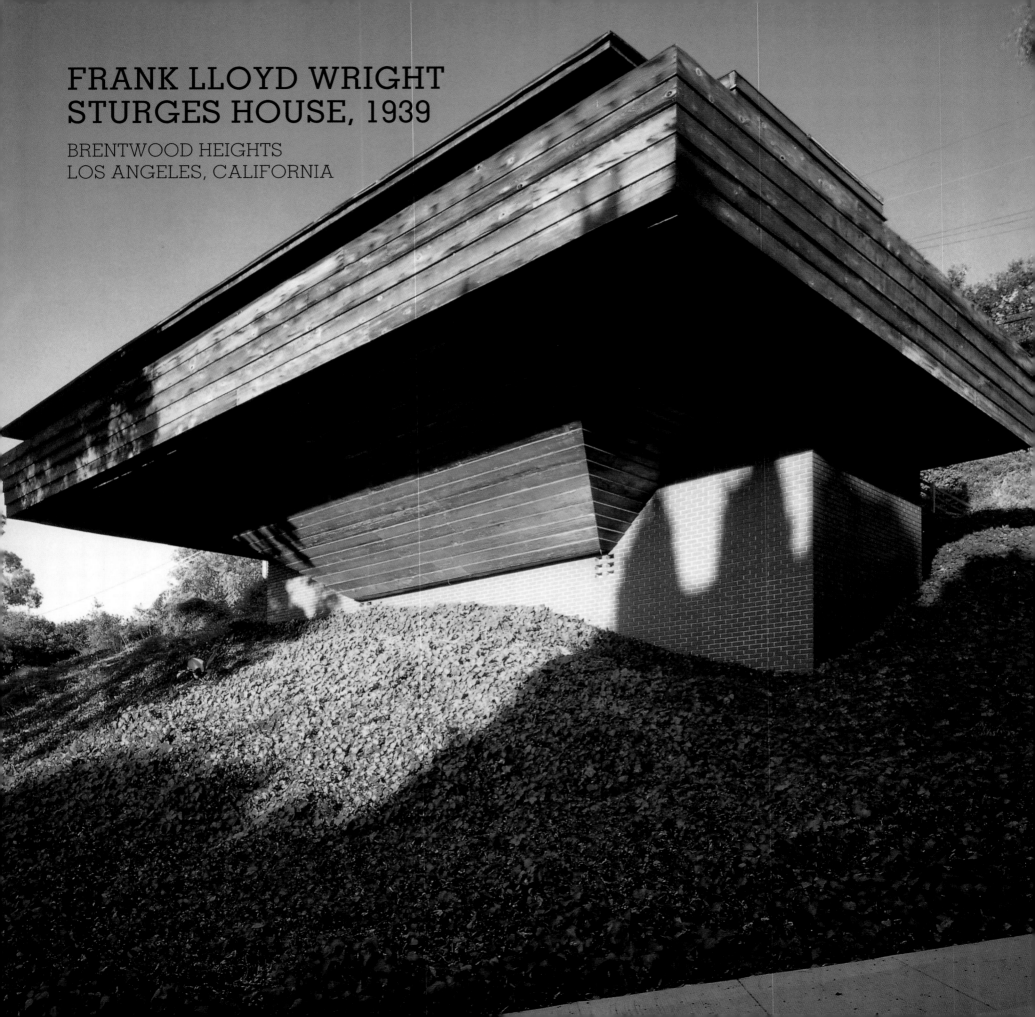

FRANK LLOYD WRIGHT
STURGES HOUSE, 1939

BRENTWOOD HEIGHTS
LOS ANGELES, CALIFORNIA

Like the Malcom Wiley House of 1932, the Sturges House contracts Wright's paradigmatic L-shaped Usonian plan into a single compact block with a large cantilevered terrace. Wright used the patent name Usonia (compounded out of utopia and U.S.A.) from the early 1930s onward to allude to an emergent middle-class American housing standard of which he was the sole progenitor. Wright had in mind a new, classless norm as applicable to the ever-expanding suburb as to the leisured estates of the rich. He based his generic Usonian plan on an economical four-by-two-foot module selected for its conformity to standard mill sizes, thereby minimizing waste. The modest cost of the Sturges House, despite its elaborate superstructure, partly resulted from the use of this module, although its total floor area of 870 square feet makes it more compact than most Usonian homes.

In the spirit of Fallingwater, the Sturges House is predicated on a seemingly extravagant cantilevered terrace that rises off a concrete foundation set into the side of a steep hill. Both house and terrace are counterweighted by a three-foot-six-inch-thick concrete wall set into the crest of the slope, into which four-by-twelve-inch timber beams are anchored. These are further braced by four-by-eight-inch diagonal stays or wailing pieces. The whole substructure is faced throughout in brick where it is concrete and in horizontal timber planking where it is wood. John Sergeant has written:

Here also the Usonian board and batten wall was varied. The plywood core was omitted and sloping studs substituted so that each external board successively lapped those below it. Unseasoned "green" redwood was used, stained rust-red. Above the roof level the boards battered inward with special bridging "drip" battens. The design has a certain inexorability, and is a terminal statement in Wright's search, stated in the 1920s, for a house that is indigenous to the Los Angeles basin.

The main approach to the house is from the east via a ramp up from the street, from which a carport and a covered walkway lead directly to the main entrance and also to the cantilevered terrace that wraps around the house on its southern and eastern sides. On the northern face, one enters directly into the living area while another door leads to the kitchen. This simple, single-story plan comprises a main living room with a built-in dining area. A corridor extends from the living room to the kitchen and then to two small bedrooms and a bathroom. As in almost all of Wright's Usonian houses, the southern face, flanking the living and sleeping spaces, is separated from an open-air terrace by large, full-height doors. This terrace gives onto a spectacular panoramic view, while the interior of the house is extremely compact and low. The wooden pergola that runs above this southern face extends the apparent volume while providing a shaded transition between the quiet interior and full glare of the sun.

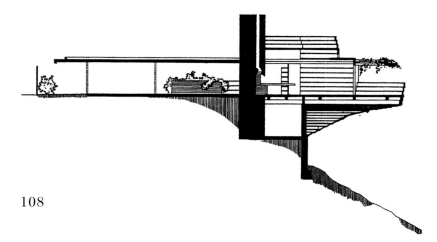

Californian redwood is the main material throughout, not only for the interior and the cantilever soffit, which appears as a gigantic timber "corbel," but also for the four-by-twelve-inch beams anchored on top of the concrete counterweight, from which the roof structure of the living room is propped up on notched timber posts. This counterweight is integral with the service zone at the back of the house, incorporating a chimney and a short stair leading down to the basement and up to the roof deck.

Aside from struck mortar joints between the horizontal courses of the brickwork and cherokee red linoleum laid on a timber floor, Wright's consummate handling of the micro-space in one transition after another testifies to his indubitable genius. This accounts for the discrete entry to the living room, via a stablelike two-leaf door that opens onto continuous built-in leather seating, which terminates in a short L in front of the doors opening onto the terrace.

Unlike the typical Usonian house, heating is provided (aside from the fireplace) by a large hot-air duct rising up from the boiler in the basement and feeding through holes in the brick lining to the

fireplace wall. Similar nuances allow for the clerestory lighting and bathroom ventilation and for the effective creation of a multilevel, timber-lined ceiling throughout that also gives the feeling of a much larger structure.

BLUEPRINT FOR MODERN LIVING:

THE AMERICAN HOUSE AND THE PAX AMERICANA 1945–1965

One of the most prophetic and elegant houses built in the United States in the early 1940s was Philip Johnson's own house (fig. 1), erected on Ash Street in Cambridge, Massachusetts, in 1942. Anticipatory of the neo-Miesianism that would dominate American architecture in the next decade, Johnson's house conveys a sense of calm that would be carried further in his Glass House, built in New Canaan, Connecticut, in 1949, and in Mies van der Rohe's Farnsworth House, built in Illinois in 1951.

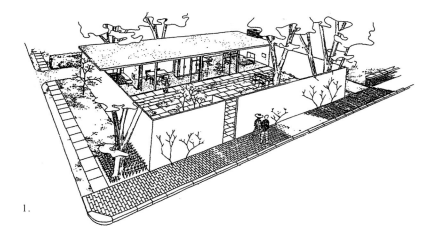

1.

Johnson's single-story Ash Street house possessed a lighter touch, however, displaying a pragmatism that anticipated the groundbreaking Southern California Case Study houses that would follow soon after. In Cambridge, Johnson employed nine-by-four-foot prefabricated plywood panels bolted together to make a continuous

perimeter enclosing both house and courtyard. Only the chimney was of masonry construction. The flat roof was built up of laminated timber beams that took their bearing from the walls and from tubular steel lally columns at midspan. The house was enclosed by a continuous plate-glass curtain wall with side-hung, full-height glazed doors, separating the interior from the stone-paved garden. The interior was a neo-Miesian exercise in spatial subdivision, largely achieved through the elegant disposition of furniture.

The Case Study program, which began in earnest in 1945 and lasted nearly twenty years, was the brainchild of John Entenza, editor of the California-based architecture magazine *Arts and Architecture*. Entenza bought the magazine in 1938 and took full control as editor two years later, redesigning it with the help of Herbert Matter and Alvin Lustig. Under the aegis of the Case Study program, the magazine was prepared to sponsor the design of certain houses, providing that it had a hand in selecting the architect and that the lot was a minimum of five acres. In addition to this, the house had to remain open to the public for a period of time after its erection. These conditions were not readily met and at times they were varied, although the basic restrictions may well explain why certain architects, such as Rudolph Schindler, Hamilton Harwell Harris, and Gregory Ain, never participated in the program. Apart from the brilliance of these houses (there were some twenty-four commissions in all), the Case Study program remains something of a historian's nightmare since the designs were often realized out of sequence and two were inexplicably given the same number.

113

The earliest canonical work was Case Study House No. 8 (1945–1949), initially designed by Charles Eames and Eero Saarinen and later re-designed by Charles and Ray Eames and realized as their home and studio. The Eames House, like Case Study House No. 9, designed for Entenza at virtually the same time (again by Eames and Saarinen), was designed to meet rather atypical requirements. Eames's intention was not to create an ideal composition but rather to assemble a set of modular forms into a free but orderly spatial relationship. As Entenza put it at the time, the Eames House represents "an attempt to state an idea rather than a fixed architectural pattern."

Of all the Case Study architects, Craig Ellwood had the most atypical career in that he entered the field through the building industry rather than through conventional training as a designer, although he was employed as a contract manager on a number of houses by Neutra, Eames, and Soriano. Ellwood's practical experience, particularly in estimating and supervising construction, equipped him with an unusual range of abilities, which he complemented by studying structural engineering at night. Thus, Ellwood acquired a profound knowledge of lightweight steel construction long before he became familiar with Mies's architecture. Ellwood opened his own office in 1948 with a commission for a number of shops and soon after he developed his own approach with the Hale House, realized between 1949 and 1951. Cradled within a steel-stilt frame on a steep slope, the Hale House was fleshed out with a wooden frame and eight-by-eight-foot sandwich plywood panels that were used for both cladding and partitioning.

Ellwood followed the Hale House with Case Study House No. 16, designed in 1951 and built in Bel Air in 1952. Seemingly derived from John Funk's Heckendorf House of 1939, this house was a study in economy and elegance. It still offered an exemplary solution to the problem of the small, single-story, steel-framed suburban house. Framed throughout in two-and-a-half-inch-square hollow columns and six-inch I-beams, the house featured remarkable full-height screens of opaque glass that imparted a sense of grandeur and radiance to a modest two-bedroom dwelling.

Ellwood's final Case Study House, No. 18, completed in 1957, is certainly the most refined of the series. Like his double-fronted Hunt House, built at the same time for the ocean front at Malibu, this structure is a minimalist tour de force. From this point onward his steel sections will become more substantial and standard and his plans

114

increasingly symmetrical, culminating in the neo-Miesian Paphne and Rosen courtyard houses of 1961 and 1963. Despite their elegance these later works followed Mies only too pendantically. Elevated off the ground like the Farnsworth House, they departed categorically from the lightweight Southern California tradition in which Ellwood had played such a seminal role.

Remote from the Case Study program, architects like Ralph Rapson, Don Knorr, and Conrad Buff displayed a discernible affinity for the early work of the young Paul Rudolph in Florida.

2.

Rudolph's Eugene Knott Residence (fig. 2), designed for Yankeetown in 1951–1952 and published by Entenza in the June 1957 issue of *Arts and Architecture*, particularly intrigued them. Conceived to be built of laminated plywood shells carried on a light steel framework, with large, rolling plate-glass walls designed to open the house to the breeze, this was as close as any non-Californian would ever come to the Case Study ethos. Created for a site at a bend in a beautiful river, this house evoked a feeling for semi-tropical luxury that not only testified to Rudolph's talent but also to the influence of Oscar Niemeyer. Regrettably, that house was never built and Rudolph never returned to such simple structural lyricism at a domestic scale, except possibly in his own townhouse realized in Manhattan in 1973.

Entenza's precipitous sale of *Arts and Architecture* in 1962 seems to have reflected the end of the euphoric postwar era not only in Southern California but elsewhere. Gropius and Breuer also seemed to lose their cutting edge at around this time. Meanwhile, the so-called New

Monumentality, which had been in the ascendancy since 1945, was somewhat unsuited to the private house as Ellwood's later work surely confirmed. Nonetheless, the New Monumentality played a prominent cultural role during the heyday of the Pax Americana between 1955 and 1965, as is evident from the work of Eero Saarinen, I. M. Pei, John Johansen, and Edward Durrell Stone during this period. Of these four only Johansen would take a more expressive and liberative stance in his domestic work, designing houses that had something in common with the experimental work of Frederick Kiesler; in particular the later's so-called Endless House.[1]

The emerging so-called Philadelphia School of the 1950s, strongly influenced by Louis Kahn's early work, predicated its domestic style on a mode of loose-fitting timber construction wrapped around a masonry core. Obvious precedents lay in Kahn's Weiss House, Norristown, Pennsylvania, of 1949, and in the diagonally inflected plan of his Fisher House, completed in Hatboro, Pennsylvania, in 1961. Both Romaldo Giurgola and Charles Moore were directly influenced by Kahn in this regard as we may judge from Giurgola's Thomas White House, built in Chestnut Hill, Philadelphia, in 1963, and from Moore's own house erected in Orinda, California, in 1961. Here Moore simultaneously alluded to the Bay Area vernacular and challenged its tradition by introducing a strict geometry of two distorted pyramidal canopies each supported on four posts and asymmetrically placed within a larger pyramidal roof. As Robert A. M. Stern has remarked, this could hardly have been further removed from Johnson's Glass House of a decade earlier, "where a virtually identical program (a bachelor architect's residence) is restricted to the confines of a box and given spatial expression through the placement of furniture."[2] Johnson himself was directly affected thereafter by the New Monumentality, abandoning the sobriety of the buildings that he had initially erected on his New Canaan estate. While modest in scale, these buildings were nonetheless extremely expressive by virtue of the opposition that they established between the crystalline character of his Glass House and the opacity of the nearby brick-faced guest house with its porthole windows. Instead of pursuing this minimalist line, Johnson gravitated in the early 1960s toward architects like Minoru Yamasaki whose pseudo-Gothic excesses appeared only too absurd when applied to the domestic scale, as in the lakeside pavilion that Johnson added to his estate in 1965.

Charles Moore's Sea Ranch complex, built in Sonoma County on a coastal bluff north of San Francisco, brings the stylistic uncertainties of the first half of the 1960s to a challenging conclusion. Clad throughout in vertical boarding with monopitched roofs and a rambling, spread-eagle plan, the Sea Ranch seems more like an agrarian settlement than a collection of duplexes. Apart from the poetic intensity of this work, designed as a team by Moore together with Donlyn Lyndon, William Turnbull, and Chris Whitaker, the Sea Ranch self-consciously reintroduced the theme of regionalism into twentieth-century American domestic architecture, an ethos that has always remained latent in this continent of widely varying climates and landscape.

While regionalism and nomadism have always been countervailing impulses in North American life, this opposition has been exacerbated in the second half of the twentieth century by the mass ownership of the automobile and the corresponding decline of the railroad. Needless to say, the introduction of universal air-conditioning has also had a homogenizing effect on American environmental cultures. Thus, the much-vaunted pluralism of the country tends to be denied by the repetitiveness of American suburban settlement as this pattern of development covers the continent from coast to coast. Even an architect as sensitive to the idiosyncrasies of climate as Wright built virtually identical Usonian houses in the Midwest and the South, despite the fact that the main thrust of "regional dissent" in American domestic architecture has largely come from former Taliesin apprentices and from various Wright sympathizers. One thinks of architects as diverse as Bruce Goff of Bartlesville, Oklahoma, John Lautner of Southern California, and Fay Jones of Arkansas. Where Goff was at his regionalist best in his circular Ford House built in Aurora, Illinois, in 1950, with its red steel structure, cedar shingles, and earthwork laid up in coal, with inset glass marbles, Lautner attained the apotheosis of his own career in his Elrod House completed in Palm Springs in 1968.

Paradoxically, given that Southern California was the one area of the nation that could boast a strong regional tradition in architecture, Lautner became an expressionist maverick. Totally disregarding the Southern California school of Soriano, Ain, Eames, and Davidson, Lautner assumed the frontier stance of the rugged individualist and built one "macho" reinforced concrete house after another. Thus, Lautner's internalization of Wright's slogan "truth before the world" led to a series of heroic domestic structures invariably made at great expense, as is all too evident from the finest work of his career, the Elrod House (fig. 3). Lautner's own description of building this house confirms the extravagance of his approach:

The original site for this residence in Palm Springs was a level "bulldozed lot" as is usual in Southern Californian subdivisions. I looked and found natural rock outcrops at the perimeter. I then requested the client cut down the ground level another eight feet to expose and then integrate these rock outcrops as part of the house.[3]

Lautner's particularly willful juxtaposition of nature and culture, plus his romantic obsession with the sovereignty of natural form, took

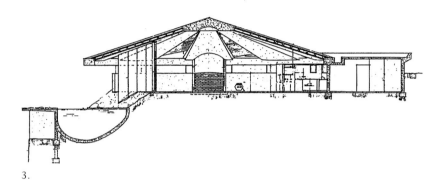

3.

him well beyond Wright's cult of the organic. Like Goff's camp reinterpretations of aboriginal Indian culture, Lautner felt compelled to indulge in gestures that, for all of their imaginative flair, invariably gravitate toward kitsch. It is hardly an accident that the apocalyptic ending of Michelangelo Antonioni's *Red Desert* takes place in a house that could have easily come from the hand of Lautner.

An entirely different and more sensitive regionalism, deriving ultimately from the Bay Area and the Northwest, was present in the early work of Josef Esherick, from his rather traditional, all timber Metcalf Vacation House built in Lake Tahoe in 1948 to his Bermak House, realized in the hills above Oakland, California, in 1963. Raised on a fairly massive concrete superstructure and elegantly assembled out of everyday materials—a standard steel spiral stair, unpainted plywood, and rough-sawn boards—this house challenges the everyday notion of modern domestic comfort with an aggressive pioneering spirit. Despite this frontier attitude, a sophisticated concatenation of horizontal wooden louvers, delicately cantilevered out into space, serves to create the crown of the house. Apart from the generosity of its inner volume, which matches the grandeur of the

surrounding panorama, the whole is touched by a certain ambiguity as Esherick would remark at the time:

What is most useful for our particular time is to produce things that are subject to a kind of ambiguity that can be interpreted in several ways. Then people are not forced to participate in a rigid, preordained way. Any environment you produce should not become dominant; people are far more important. The very ambiguity of the social science problem, and I take design to be a social science problem, its woolliness, its vagueness, all of these elements of the problem are in fact elements of life itself. Our design must preserve this capacity for ambiguity.[4]

We cannot recall the 1960s without mentioning Sergei Chermayeff and Christopher Alexander's *Community and Privacy*, published in 1963. Without displaying any particular concern for the single-family house, this text nonetheless critically addressed the imminent future of the American suburb and proposed an alternative land settlement pattern that would be capable of yielding higher densities. Forerunner of the so-called low-rise high-density principle, *Community and Privacy* postulated a new type of courtyard house specially designed so as to be economical while at the same time accommodating within the unit itself a spatial allocation that would have been appropriate to the separate needs of the different family members. Chermayeff and Robert Reynolds first developed their long, generic single-story courtyard house (fig. 4) with an entrance at either end, for a narrow plot in Cambridge, Massachusetts, in 1957. Chermayeff built a similar prototype for his own occupation in New Haven, Connecticut, in 1962.

This generic prototype was a twenty-foot-wide house set between solid cross-walls and comprised of three dwelling zones separated from one another by diminutive patios. The adult zone, entered from one end, contained a master bedroom and patio, a bath, and a living room. The second zone comprised the family/television room, while the last zone, entered from the other end, housed the children's bedrooms and bathroom. Additional patios, back and front, were provided to buffer the sleeping areas from pedestrian access ways. In the early 1960s a student study team led by Peter Chermayeff produced a plan for twenty houses of thirty-one hundred square feet each laid out in closely packed clusters, yielding a density of forty-one houses per acre. While this layout was particularly dense, Yale University students working under Chermayeff's direction produced more moderate and varied low-rise, suburban formations, such as a particularly ingenious variation on the 1934 Stein and Wright Radburn principle designed by

Der Scutt, yielding a density of thirty-six houses per acre (fig. 5). If Wright's Usonian house thirty years before was the last attempt to render the suburb as a place of middle-class culture, *Community and Privacy* was the last effort to postulate a more ecologically valid, suburban land settlement pattern readily accessible to middle-class users of varying incomes. This new megalopolitan norm would have entailed a radical change in our current modes of subdividing and zoning land; a price that, in terms of individual freedom, we have so far been unwilling to pay.

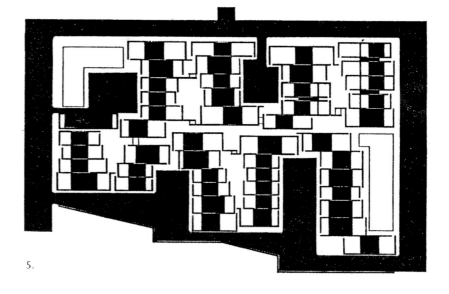

5.

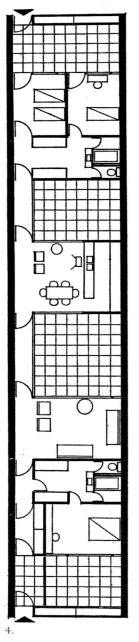

4.

RICHARD NEUTRA
KAUFMANN HOUSE, 1946

PALM SPRINGS, CALIFORNIA

Built in the so-called Badlands, when the desert resort of Palm Springs barely existed, this thirty-eight-hundred-square-foot house was conceived as a prefabricated, lightweight oasis set down in the midst of a hostile desert. With the exception of its first-floor belvedere, backed up against the sublime panorama of the San Jacinto mountain range, this was a single-story structure organized around a forty-by-fifty-foot living room, together with a forty-five-foot-long swimming pool and terrace set to one side a few feet below the general datum. The continuous living volume extended eastward to embrace a dining area overlooking a patio-deck terminated by a guest wing and a thirty-seven-foot-long louvered screen wall made of aluminum blades, which were set against the prevailing northwesterly wind. Flanked throughout its length by a water channel filled with lilies, this screen was typical of Neutra's approach to passive environmental control. Like the similarly louvered belvedere above, this screen protected the patio from sandstorms while helping to sustain a naturally humidified and cooled microclimate.

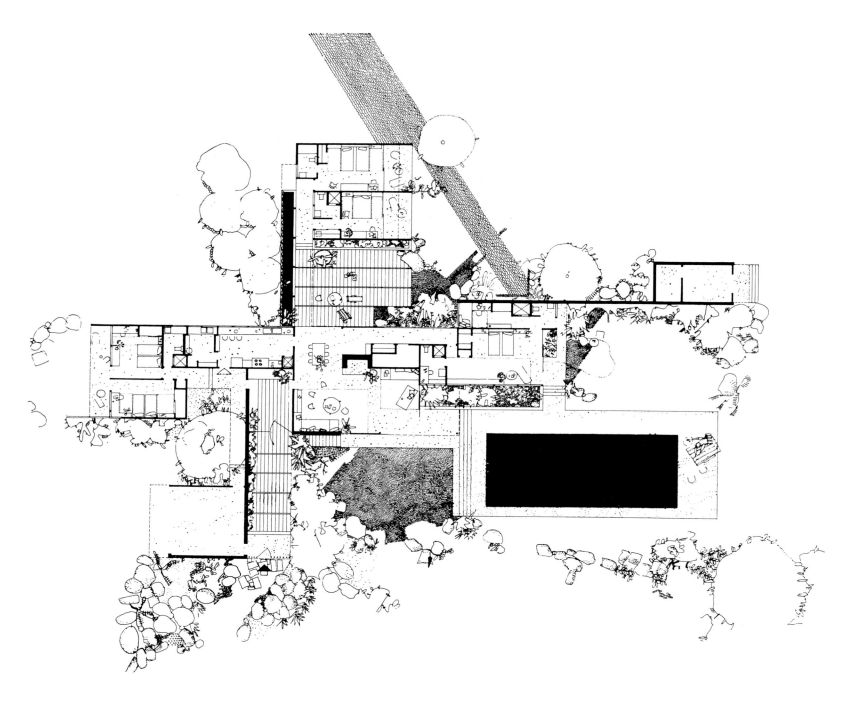

While its spread-eagle swastika plan occupied nearly a quarter of the available site, its actual accommodation in terms of built volume was relatively small, comprising, in addition to the living core, two self-contained guest bedrooms each with its own bathroom and terrace, a master bedroom suite with separate dressing and bathing facilities, and an independent kitchen/servant wing extending westward out of the living volume. Two outriding, long walls, at right angles to each other, in addition to the patio screen wall, formed the countervailing arms of the rest of the plan, with one wall flanking a covered entryway to the south and the other terminating in a single-story

electrical switch room to the east. As would often be the case in Neutra's houses, the ultimate centroid of the dwelling was a freestanding chimney, clad in masonry, that rose up through the middle of the living volume to serve the auxiliary living space of the so-called gloriette above, a heat source to offset the coldness of the desert air at night. This feature, rising up as a solid four-square block of masonry above both the house and the gloriette, provided a solid core against the silver metal trim and dematerialized walls of the house.

No one has perhaps characterized the circumstances leading to the creation of this house more succinctly than Thomas Hines who, in his 2005 study of Neutra, wrote:

. . . Edgar Kaufmann, a wealthy Pittsburgh merchant and philanthropist, was already famous in architectural circles for commissioning Frank Lloyd Wright in 1936 to design his epochal Fallingwater vacation house near Pittsburgh. Kaufmann's son Edgar, Jr., an architect, historian, and fond disciple of Wright's, wanted his father to engage Wright again to design the new Palm Springs winter house, but the senior Kaufmann, while a warm admirer of Wright, wanted for the desert house a greater feeling of lightness and openness than Wright had imparted either to Fallingwater or to his own "desert house" at Taliesin West. For this new commission he found Neutra the most interesting prospect. It was not unlike Philip Lovell's decision some twenty years earlier to move from Rudolph Schindler, the designer of his beach house, to Neutra, who was the architect of his house in the city. Whatever the motivations in each of the two cases for moving to Neutra as the second architect, the results were salutary. In both cases the clients not only bought great houses for their personal enjoyment, but also contributed richly to architecture.

Despite the full-height, plate-glass walls of the living room, which at the southeastern corner could be mutually slid back so as to completely dematerialize the enclosure, Neutra offset the lightweight, metallic character of the house with natural materials; in particular, the redwood decking and ceiling of the "gloriette" and the buff Dakota sandstone used to clad the chimney and face the four-by-two-inch stud wall, lined with plywood, which flanks one side of the covered entry into the house. The varying depth of masonry coursework and the rough-cut character of the stone were surely intended to recall Wright's similar use of stone veneer in Fallingwater. At the same time, the sybaritic aura of the house, its sunbathing terraces and its well-manicured lawns overlooked by both the living room and the master bedroom, conveyed a sense of hedonism, which would be perfectly captured in the photographs of Julius Shulman working under Neutra's direction. As Hines reminds us: "*The picture taken from the east of the house and pool at twilight would become, in particular, one of modern architecture's most brilliant and famous photographs. Shulman's interpretations were widely published, and the house was internationally acclaimed.*"

127

The Farnsworth House is one of the most remarkable and mysterious works of this century. Pragmatically, it is the reductio ad absurdum of the notion of dwelling. At the same time, it is a work of metaphysical beauty. Perhaps the single most misleading factor in our perception of it is its size, for while it comprises an enclosed area of something over one thousand square feet, it occupies a seemingly much larger volume.

Situated forty-seven miles west of Chicago in Plano, Illinois, on a flood plain adjacent to the Fox River, this house was built as a weekend retreat for Dr. Edith Farnsworth, who first met Mies van der Rohe in 1947. The house finally took shape conceptually after a long period of gestation, during which time a personal relationship developed between architect and client. This intimacy began to erode soon after the house went into construction in 1949, and on its completion in 1951 the friendship had so deteriorated that the architect sued the client and client the architect in a bitter dispute that was finally settled in the architect's favor. While the house was warmly received by critics all over the world, Mies suffered almost as much as his client from the negative publicity and subsequently refused to accept domestic commissions.

To a greater degree than the Barcelona Pavilion of 1929 to which it is clearly related, the house is planned on a strict two-foot square grid that also conforms to the unit size of the square travertine paving slabs that cover both the house and its outside terraces, the one intimately linked to the main body of the house and the other placed somewhat lower as an approach platform. The house and its platforms are suspended above the site on steel stanchions, simplifying the entire work to three horizontal planes: platform, main floor, and roof. The vertical supports are equally minimal, consisting of twelve steel stanchions that carry the three planes, eight supporting the main body of the house and four carrying the outer perimeter of the platform. A double flight of low, travertine-covered stairs connects the ground to the platform and the platform to the covered terrace.

131

The whole is made up of exposed, welded, steel-frame construction onto which all the other elements are applied. The floors, roof, and fixed plate-glass walls are held in place by light steel fenestration. Given this hermetic approach to enclosure and the proximity of the river, it is odd that the house is not air-conditioned, particularly since this could have been installed through the floor or the roof without seriously affecting the general appearance of the house. One can only assume that for Mies such a provision would have compromised the fundamental purity of the tectonic frame, although even this is odd given that he readily accepted such technology in most of his American work.

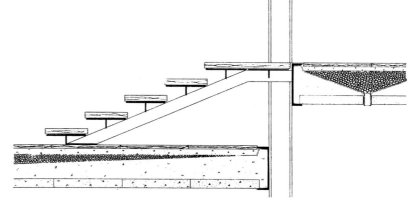

Aesthetically speaking, the house is full of subtle nuances that are easily missed if one is not attentive to the particularly delicate adjustments that occur throughout. Such refinements appear in the absolutely flat paved terraces that require special drainage. The terraces incorporate inverted, pyramidal drain pans in welded sheet steel that drain surface water from the joints between the paving slabs. Mies pursued this standard of absolute precision further by grinding all the welds flat, sandblasting the steel, and painting the exposed frame white. The glass box itself is effectively bracketed and sustained by six columns, while the approach platform and the house and its terrace are jointly carried by six and eight stanchions each. In each instance the columns are eight modules apart longitudinally, with two cantilevers (four feet or two slabs) at the extremities in the longitudinal direction. In the other direction the inside face of the steel sits flush-faced against the perimeter of the roof and the lower terrace. With consummate skill, inducing a minor/major reading across the overall section, the lower terrace is three modules narrower than the house, yielding a depth of twenty feet versus the twenty-six feet of the house.

The main space is served and activated by a single, elongated wood-paneled core that accommodates a kitchen on one side and a hearth on the other and two full bathrooms at either end, one for the entry foyer and one for the sleeping area. The latter is separated from the living space by a matching, freestanding clothes closet. In a play between these wood-faced elements, the core rises up to the ceiling and the closet stops short.

The rest of the open space is orchestrated by the careful placement of Mies's own furniture: three Barcelona chairs and attendant stools, and a narrow dining table with four MR50 Brno chairs. Contrary to myth, however, the number and placement of these pieces does not accord with any absolute principle.

135

Despite its simplicity, this minimalist work is of considerable cultural complexity. The house evokes diverse references, including the elided asymmetrical form of the Italianate villas that Karl Friedrich Schinkel designed for Potsdam. The integration of the house with nature is perhaps of a more recent provenance, although here too the mode of beholding relates to the German aesthetic tradition, as Wolf Tegethoff has demonstrated in his study of Mies's villas published in 1957. Tegethoff convincingly argues that the nature/culture relationship in the Farnsworth House derives from Mies's earlier Resor House, projected for Jackson Hole, Wyoming, in 1937. Both of these houses provide vantage points from which to behold the beauty of natural form from a distance. Tegethoff has written of the Resor House:

The deliberate transformation of the landscape into a picture is the necessary prerequisite for the increasing openness of Miesian space. For only in this way can the interior maintain its identity and integrity, provide shelter and security, and nevertheless convey a feeling of freedom. Without this scenic backdrop that "closes" the room, it would expand into the infinite, which would be tantamount to its total dissolution. Solely its having been "set apart" guarantees its separate existence.

For his part, Mies gave a clear indication of his attitude to nature when he wrote:

Nature should also have a life of its own. We should avoid disturbing it with the excessive color of our houses, and our interior furnishings. Indeed, we should strive to bring Nature, houses and people together into a higher unity. When one looks at Nature through the glass walls of the Farnsworth House it takes on a deeper significance than when one stands outside. More of Nature is thus expressed— it becomes part of a greater whole.

This all but mystical view of nature invites comparison to the highest achievements of Shinto culture and at the same time to the modern, dematerializing sensibility as this may be found in the work of such artists as Kasimir Malevich and Ad Reinhardt. And yet while this house is unquestionably a work of art, it may well be that only a bachelor's retreat can really constitute the legitimate basis for such an exercise, as Philip Johnson would demonstrate in his own version of the concept realized in New Canaan, Connecticut, in 1949.

PHILIP JOHNSON
GLASS HOUSE, 1949

NEW CANAAN, CONNECTICUT

The most surprising thing about Philip Johnson's Glass House is not so much that it derives from the Farnsworth House as that it remains relatively independent of Mies's influence. While virtually unthinkable without the Miesian precedent, the Glass House also displays a phenomenological character quite removed from the Miesian ethos. This is evident in a number of ways, most notably in the particular relationship that it establishes with the site and with the natural environment. Unlike the Farnsworth House, which is closer in its setting to the work of Schinkel and to the picturesque sensibility of Uvedale Price, Johnson's Glass House displays an affinity for the genteel vision of Capability Brown. Thus, Johnson treats the greensward surrounding his house as a manicured lawn on which are arranged a series of objects, large and small. In the Farnsworth House, opposing forms slide past each other within a single whole, but in Johnson's house the dialogue turns on two contrasting buildings arranged around the sides of an implicit space; the one, the main house, being fully glazed and the other, the guest house, being brick-faced and largely opaque. These forms are set off from each other by diagonal paths cut in the grass, while three other elements completed the initial composition: a freestanding sculpture by Jacques Lipchitz, a circular reflecting pool, and the remains of an ivy-covered fieldstone wall running across the site. Johnson cited the nineteenth-century French theorist Auguste Choisy's interpretation of the Athenian acropolis as an inspiration for this assembly.

This topographic aesthetic continues inside the house, for unlike the Farnsworth House, the surroundings seem to enter almost as physical presences into the living volume, in part because of the proximity of the carpetlike brick podium to the level of the lawn, but also because of the proportions of the space in relation to the furnishings that subdivide its volume into bar, dining area, and zones for living and sleeping. This *paysagiste* sensibility is consummated by two works of art, a painting and a large figurative sculpture that complete the garden metaphor and relate to other objects in the surrounding landscape. Here the surrounding planting seems at times to be literally inscribed on the surface of the glass, when seen from within or, alternatively, when seen from without, the same foliage may be transformed into a filigree of reflections.

Influenced by the Schinkelesque paradigm of the patio and the belvedere, as this couple had been ambiguously played with in all of Mies's German houses of the 1930s, Johnson opted to treat his house as a glass box within a virtual court, which may account for the suppression of the house's steel structure by merging its steel stanchions with the lighter bar-steel of its fenestration. Nothing could be further from the Farnsworth House than this picturesque detail, for while the four H-sections at the corners of the box are inevitably expressed, the intermediate stanchions are virtually hidden.

Where the stanchions of the Farnsworth House stress the isolated horizontal planes of its floor and ceiling and hence the distant vista infinitely extending out between them, Johnson's Glass House is focused about a brick cylinder that pierces the roof slab. At the same

time the brick herringbone pattern of the podium floor fuses with the brick cylinder of the bathroom/chimney core. This image, drawn from Johnson's memory of an incinerated house, becomes the main focus of the work. As Johnson put it in 1950:

The cylinder, made of the same brick as the platform from which it springs, forming the main motif of the house, was not derived from Mies, but rather from a burnt-out wooden village I saw once where nothing was left but the foundations and chimneys of brick. Over the chimney I slipped a steel cage with a glass skin. The chimney forms the anchor.

This unexpected traditional weight placed in the center of the house is countered by the lightness of its skin, which depends for its Oriental effect on the raw silk screens that slide on tracks inside the glass to protect the interior from sunlight. This feeling for technological dematerialization attains its apotheosis when it snows, whereupon, as the architect once remarked, the house resembles a "celestial elevator."

CHARLES AND RAY EAMES
EAMES HOUSE, CASE STUDY HOUSE NO. 8, 1945–1949

PACIFIC PALISADES, LOS ANGELES, CALIFORNIA

The December 1945 issue of John Entenza's magazine *Arts and Architecture* featured two house projects designed by Charles Eames in association with Eero Saarinen. The first of these houses, also then known as Case Study House No. 8, was designed for Eames's own occupation; the second, Case Study House No. 9, was to be Entenza's home. The two were sited in close proximity to each other on a three-acre plot in the Palisades. The Entenza House lay with a hill running behind it along its western edge, whereas the Eames House was raised up on the hill overlooking the ocean.

Three years later Eames abandoned the neo-Miesian bridge house of the initial project (reminiscent of Mies's 1934 sketch for a hillside house that Eames later saw at the Museum of Modern Art in 1947) and opted instead for a house plus studio set parallel to the lower contours of the hill. This radical last-minute revision, prompted in part by his break with Saarinen, occurred after the steel for the first version had already been delivered to the site.

Eames was sufficiently ingenious to reuse the same steel in constructing the new design. According to Eduardo Contini, who served as structural engineer for both houses, Eames abandoned the initial scheme because it "resembled too closely an extant building of Saarinen's." Ray Eames has suggested that the revised design was partly based on winning entries for the "Design for Postwar Living" competition organized by *Arts and Architecture* in 1943.

As built, the Eames House is distinguished by the uncanny simplicity and elegance of its space-form, broken down at grade level from left to right into living terrace, living room, sitting alcove, darkroom, and studio. The living room and studio are double-height volumes at either end of this linear assembly, with each featuring a raised gallery at the second floor. The living room mezzanine is a sleeping loft comprising two bedrooms, with bathroom and walk-in closets attached, whereas the upper level in the studio provides storage space.

The house backs up against a concrete retaining wall that also serves to unify the entire scheme. The rest of the structure consists of an exposed steel frame, comprising I-section columns set at seven-foot-six-inch centers and tied longitudinally by twelve-inch-deep channels and cross-braced on the eastern wall with steel rods. Each frame supports twelve-inch-deep exposed lattice girders in the transverse direction that carry the exposed ribbed steel decking of the roof and first floor. Eames articulated this skeleton through the structural use of color, as he explained in 1949:

Color was planned and used as a structural element, and while much concern was given to its use in various structural planes, the most gratifying of all the painted surfaces is the dark, warm gray that covers the structural steel and the metal sash. The varying thickness and the constant strength of this line does more than anything else to express what goes on in the structural web that surrounds the building. It is also this gray web that holds in a unity the stucco panels of white, blue, red, black, and earth.

The cladding of this skeleton frame suggests a textile: the "warp" of the frame interweaving with the "weft" of the horizontal mullions and window sashes, which are filled with glass, wood, or plaster. The larger, solid areas of the infill are either metal decking set vertically or

plaster on metal lath. Unlike Mies van der Rohe's trabeated frames, where the steel stanchions are invariably capped by an entablature, here the woven membrane continues right up to within three inches of the thin, built-up roof.

The result is a lightweight dwelling constructed largely from off-the-shelf steel window sashes and open-web joists. Almost everything installed within is either fair-faced or finished with wood veneer or painted board. The facades are subtle compositions of transparent and translucent glass set against infill panels painted in primary colors. The quality of light inside changes constantly due to the glass and to the shadows cast by the surrounding foliage. There is something Japanese about this house that cannot be truly accounted for in stylistic terms. Furnished with a few classic pieces designed by Eames, the interior is enriched by a collage of non-Western carpets and folk objects that Eames collected on his travels. In this popular appraisal of folk culture and in its deadpan application of technology, the Eames House had an extensive influence, informing European high-tech architecture, as well as a later generation of Southern California architects, particularly in the late 1970s in the work of Helmut Schulitz and Peter de Bretteville.

146

CRAIG ELLWOOD
CASE STUDY HOUSE NO. 16, 1952–1953

BEL AIR, CALIFORNIA

Craig Ellwood's two-bedroom Case Study House No. 16, built in 1953, is the first of three houses that he designed under the auspices of the *Arts and Architecture* magazine Case Study program. Situated on a flat parcel of land in the Bel Air hills, the house has sweeping views to the west and the south.

Ellwood's background as an engineer/contractor and his lack of formal training as an architect enabled him to indulge in uninhibited experimentation. As he put it, "I was never tied to standard detailing or inhibited from trying out new methods. When you haven't been taught that some detail is impossible, you approach it with confidence and innocence which works in your favor."

Predicated on a four-foot square module (to accord with the standard mill dimensions), the flat roof of this single-story house rests on a grid of two-and-a-half-inch square tubular columns, at eight-foot centers, with six-inch-deep I-beams spanning between. The frame is expressed by exposing the columns together with the lower half of the I-beams. As a result, certain interior partitions are treated as floating vertical planes that disengage from both the floor and the ceiling. Ellwood achieved this effect by recessing the baseboard and by placing a transom of glass at the top of the wall, creating a clerestory strip that could be left open. Ellwood was also able to contrast the exposed steel structure with wall panels that are warmer in texture and feeling, usually made of wood veneers or colored laminated surfaces. To mediate the transparency of the house in an urban setting, Ellwood provided steel-framed translucent glass screens that define the boundaries of the garden as well as those of the viewing terraces along the southern edge of the site. Along the eastern approach boundary the house is shielded from the street by translucent screens. As Amelia Jones and Elizabeth Smith have written:

The definition of walls as almost free-standing units, which was emphasized by the red painted steel members that define the decisions of the basic grid, is further dramatized by the translucent panels separating the bedroom's outdoor courtyards from the street. These screen-like walls, which also appear to hover effortlessly, provide privacy and allow luminous patterns of plant and human forms to filter out from within the house quarters. At night these walls can be backlit for a striking theatrical effect—visually transforming the solid house into a radiantly shimmering field of light.

This house is remarkable for the unusual fluidity and generosity of its space, particularly as one passes from the living volume out toward the west, through the open kitchen/dining corner, to culminate in a reflecting pool and a patio built up out of large concrete slabs and covered by a red steel pergola.

This house is a prologue to Ellwood's two other Case Study houses, nos. 17 and 18, built in the late 1950s and now altered beyond all recognition by time and vandalism. In No. 18, with its dimensionless flat roof, Ellwood took Eames's and Soriano's dematerialization to its ultimate conclusion.

CHARLES MOORE, DONLYN LYDON,
WILLIAM TURNBULL & CHRIS WHITAKER
SEA RANCH CONDOMINIUM, 1964–1965

SONOMA COUNTY, CALIFORNIA

Composed of a series of housing units clustered in such a way as to resemble a small village, the Sea Ranch consists of a number of taut geometrical forms grouped around an external courtyard and an adjacent auto court. Most of these dwellings have chimneys or belvederes marking the highest point of their monopitched roofs. In addition to the continuous sweeping form of the roof alignments, the architects gave careful consideration to the juxtaposition of materials and windows. Relatively large, with minimal molding, trim, and mullions, these provide uninterrupted views of the landscape and ocean beyond. Some of this fenestration projects outside the main envelope and is equipped with external canvas awnings to shade the openings from the sun. The entire complex is clad in vertical wooden siding with shingled roofs. These wall and roof surfaces are of similar texture and color, and the elimination of trim enables the entire mass to be read as one continuous sculptural form. Of the elemental character of this complex Henry Plummer has written:

From its first ecological conception Sea Ranch was carefully planned to preserve, even intensify, a desolate and brooding ocean site. The early condominium, in particular, has avoided domesticating the ragged bluffs along the shore by concentrating into a shape as raked and windswept as the surrounding terrain. Buildings are made out of primitive matter . . . fashioned out of massive and brutish timber frames, their elements unselfconsciously tied together with exposed joints, metal connectors, and bolts, then clad with vertical redwood boards left to weather like driftwood, battered by winds and salty *spray, making the complex as elemental and genuine as the old wooden barns nearby, or the coarse shacks of mining and timber sites in the region. Untended grasses and bedrock run right up to walls, and the complex is positioned into the most alive and dangerous regions of space out on the very brink of the cliffs . . .*

The structuring of the dwelling turns upon the articulation of a timber frame that by virtue of its square and circular sections returns us to the ethos of vernacular construction. This undressed frame is used to establish the main living volume of each duplex—the so-called "great room"—as well as to delineate smaller living volumes such as the kitchen/bathroom core, stacked on two floors, and the main sleeping platform raised up on four cylindrical posts. Beneath this square form lies the hearth-space; there are two other sitting/work spaces to either side, apart from the dining area with its circular table seating six people.

The interior organization is treated like a house within a house, with the timber core being painted various shades of gray in contrast to the unpainted timber of the external walls and the exposed frame. Plummer compares this to the duality that obtains between a shaggy outer garment and its velvet inner lining. All in all there is an Oriental, not to say, Turkish atmosphere about the way the interiors are furnished.

Nomadism is implicit here and is playfully combined with a marine-cum-camping metaphor that suffuses the interior. Somewhere between a treehouse and a ship's bunk, the sleeping mezzanine with its four-square canvas hood hanging from a skylight above also evokes the notion of a desert tent under the stars. In this way this Gaston Bachelard–like retreat set on the very edge of the Pacific remains after thirty years the single most poetic work to come from the hands of these architects.

156

COMPLEXITY AND CONTRADICTION:

THE LATE-MODERN HOUSE
1965–2007

While Kahn clearly influenced the younger Philadelphia architects such as Robert Venturi and Romaldo Giurgola, neither was a direct pupil. Venturi and Kahn shared a feeling for the way in which the oblique could be introduced into the orthogonal plan in order to effect dynamic spatial displacements in what would have otherwise been a rather banal domestic format. This subversive strategy is already evident in Venturi's Pearson House project of 1957 and in his Beach House proposal of two years later. The latter further reflects the Kahnian device of a building within a building or, let us say, within a skin, thereby exploiting the hermetic nature of the balloon frame as this had already appeared in the Shingle Style. In fact, this house was to have been faced entirely in shingles, except for the brick buttressed chimney. Venturi's description of this project sets the stage for the Shingle Style revival that followed:

The walls are balloon frame. The roof is wood-plank, toenailed so that the whole structure is a skin and a quasi-frame at the same time. An exception occurs at the inverse clerestory and at the front opening, where the span is exceptionally long, and where there are some expedient frame members: one post and some beams. This exception at the center makes the overall skin structure more apparent. (The floor is raised on wood piles and beams.) . . . The whole outside surface is natural cedar shingles. Barge boards at the juncture of the roof and wall are minimized to make roof and wall look more continuous. The overlapping scales of the walls end in a skirt over the piles. Windows and porch openings punch varying holes in the continuous skin. The interior surfaces, which you see beyond the windows and within the porch, are contrastingly painted board surfaces, like the inside lining of a cape. The soffits of the openings, where the skin is cut, are painted a contrasting color. The shingles never touch the block chimney and its buttress, which divides near its base, and forms an open vestibule as well.[1]

Yet neither the ensuing Shingle Style nor Venturi himself ever quite equaled the didactic elegance of this small, canonical project. After attempting to pursue the Beach House proposal in similar houses, none of which were ever realized, Venturi finally built a house along these lines for his mother in Chestnut Hill, Pennsylvania, in 1964 (fig. 1). Venturi retained from the Beach House project the central chimney/entry axis and the particular focus on the hearth through the use of a diagonal. In this ultra-compact plan he saw the chimney and the stair as rival elements competing for the same space in the center of the house, each having to distort a little in respect of the other. Vincent Scully likened these mutually inflected elements to the bent walls and built-in seating of Wilson Eyre's Shingle Style Potter House, built nearby in Chestnut Hill, in 1886.

Scully's 1974 survey of the neo–Shingle Style, *The Shingle Style Today*, included a number of rising architects, among them, Frank Israel, Richard Weinstein, Jacqueline Robertson, Richard Saul Wurman, Giovanni Pasanella, and Romaldo Giurgola. Some of these architects had been apprenticed to Edward Larrabee Barnes and were thus also indirectly influenced by the work of Marcel Breuer. While Scully particularly valued the architecture of Charles Moore and Robert Venturi together with the promise of Robert Stern's pool house in

1.

159

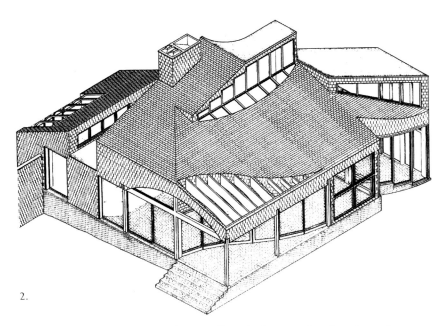

2.

Greenwich, Connecticut, of 1973 (fig. 2), he saw the Shingle Style revival as also including certain neo-Cubist works, such as the cedar-sided house that Gwathmey designed for his parents in 1967 and even Giurgola's white-sided Dayton House, built in Wayzata near Minneapolis, in 1970. The apotheosis of Scully's critical anthology are the Trubek and Wislocki houses built on Nantucket in 1972 (fig. 3) to the designs of Venturi and Rauch. These twin forms recall, despite their mannered fenestration, the subtly inflected but traditional saltbox forms employed by Eleanor Raymond in her Gloucester Harbor compound, built some thirty years before.

Of these taut, shingle-sided "dumb and ordinary" Nantucket vacation houses, Scully wrote:

With the Trubek and Wislocki houses we are in the presence of what modern architects have always said they most wanted: a true vernacular architecture—common, buildable, traditional in the deepest sense, and of piercing symbolic power. It is the bread and the wine united to the sublime as sustenance no less than symbol. But architects have mostly

3.

not really wanted a vernacular at all, lest it cut them out. They are, like all modern artists, necessarily restless men. The architects of the new Shingle Style are not less so, despite their disenchantment with "progress" and their sympathy for the vernacular forms. Therefore—if I may be allowed a minor prophecy of very short range—many of them seem to be moving (though perhaps not their younger students, such as Brooks and others) much as the architects of the first Shingle Style moved: toward a somewhat more cubical, perhaps a more "classicizing" kind of design. Not, it must be said, toward either McKim, Mead and White's literal classicism of precedent, or Wright's strict order of integrated type and progressive development, but toward something much more like the work of Lutyens, which eventually tended toward a kind of classicism too, but which remained varied and eclectic, and in a sense refused to "progress" or to tighten up into a closed system.[2]

With this perceptive insight, the postmodern line was seen as being fully available, for while Scully was in one sense only reaffirming his earlier acclaim of the American tradition, he was in another distancing himself from those aspects of the same tradition that could be associated with the European avant-garde, particularly as this non-American stance was then being embraced by the so-called Five Architects, and, to a lesser degree perhaps, by the veteran CIAM architect José Luis Sert at Harvard. In adopting such a position Scully prepared the ground for the subsequent transformation of the neo–Shingle Style into a kind of pseudo-classical pastiche that attained its scenographic nadir in Charles Moore's Piazza d'Italia, built in New Orleans in 1979.

The loose association known as the Five Architects first came to the fore with the publication of the book *Five Architects: Eisenman, Graves, Gwathmey, Hejduk, Meier* in 1972. What all these architects had in common, at the time, was an intense commitment to the formal syntax of the European architectural avant-garde between the two world wars. Assuming neo-avant-gardist positions equally distant from both the technocratic neo-Miesianism of the Chicago School and the neo–Shingle Style revisionism of the East Coast, Michael Graves, Charles Gwathmey, and Richard Meier based their early work on loose interpretations of Le Corbusier's Purist architecture of the late 1920s. The remaining members of the group, Peter Eisenman and John Hejduk, turned toward more arcane manifestations within the prewar European avant-garde, with Eisenman investigating the work of the Italian rationalist architect Giuseppe Terragni and Hejduk turning to the work of Dutch neo-Plastic painter/architect Theo Van Doesburg.

Pragmatically, each of the Five Architects assumed quite different criteria for the design of domestic space. Thus, where Gwathmey adopted a dynamically rhythmic approach to proportioning and furnishing the residential interior, Hejduk embraced a more hermetic and emblematic attitude, even at his most empirical, in such works as his Bernstein and Bye houses of the 1960s. It is to be regreted that none of the houses John Hejduk designed in the second half of the 1960s came to fruition. Hejduk's penchant for metaphysical abstraction is evident in his House 10 of 1966 (fig. 4), where the graphic mode of representation is as much part of the artistic concept as the planimetric arrangement of space.

Such designs evidently tended toward being intellectual exercises more than realistic propositions. This tendency to conceive of the house as a building without a program also appeared in Eisenman's early works, such as House II, realized for Richard Falk in Vermont, which was more of an abstract model built full size than a dwelling

layered, Graves introduces a baroque element into his reinterpretation of the Corbusian syntax. At this stage in his development, virtually every house had a mural at its center from which the layered, planar, and eroded space of the house seemed to emanate outward. There was also something highly topographic about his work at this time— a concern for the integration of the house with the landscape that reached its apotheosis in the Rockefeller House designed for Pocantico Hills, New York, in 1969. Graves returned to this theme, in a minor key, in the Crooks and Shulman houses designed for Princeton in 1976. Soon after, however, he abandoned this Piranesian reinterpretation of modern themes in favor of a pseudo-classical pastiche that has prevailed in his domestic work since the late 1970s.

The 1970s saw the emergence of a number of fresh talents across the country, starting in the Southwest with Antoine Predock, who received his first commission on graduating from Columbia University in 1967. Between 1967 and 1971 Predock realized La Luz,

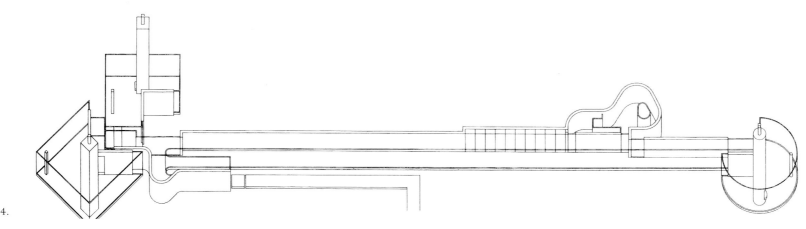

4.

conceived in pragmatic terms. If not itself a manifesto, House II provided the occasion for one, that is to say for Eisenman's "Cardboard Architecture: House II," as published in *Five Architects*. Here Eisenman revealed his preoccupation with an architectural autonomy that had an essentially musical, not to say frugal, character. This was substantiated by his insistence on establishing a basic condition that is subsequently transformed by a series of formal permutations.

Such abstract concerns were foreign to the early domestic work of Richard Meier and Michael Graves, as we may tell from the only too-sober plan of Meier's Smith House, built in Darien, Connecticut, in 1965, or from Graves's equally reasonable Hanselman House built in Fort Wayne, Indiana, in 1967. Where the Smith House is frontal and

a clustered development comprising some twenty-one adobe houses on a mesa overlooking the Rio Grande, approximately twelve miles northwest of Albuquerque, New Mexico. Built largely of adobe block and then finished in reddish brown stucco, La Luz is carefully layered into its site. Beyond its status as speculative housing, it provided Predock with an occasion for realizing a form that was precisely related to the surrounding landscape of scrub and dry grass extending from the mesa to the water's edge. La Luz demonstrated how land could be improved rather than despoiled by development.

It also showed how housing units could be clustered without losing their individuality. Organized so that half of the houses face east across a semi-arid mesa to a tree-lined flood plain, La Luz is made up

161

of split-level houses in which each room has its own view. As it stands the units overlook one another as they step down the mesa, while outriding parapet walks screen out the immediate environment in favor of the mountains beyond. Thus Predock, in his first commission, organically realized what Chermayeff and Alexander had theoretically formulated a decade earlier in *Community and Privacy*. While this work also established Predock as a "regionalist" architect, a critical stance has sustained his work to date by enabling him to achieve a wide range of site-sensitive works. In the late 1980s these included a number of villas that were intimately related to the desert.

Predock's architecture derives in part from the work of the Mexican architect Luis Barragán and his follower Ricardo Legorreta. Barragán's minimalist vernacular style first emerged in 1947 in his own house (fig. 5), built in the Tacubaya district of Mexico City.

Barragán's introspective approach came into its own with La Pedregal, an upper-class garden suburb set in a wild volcanic outcrop. Here

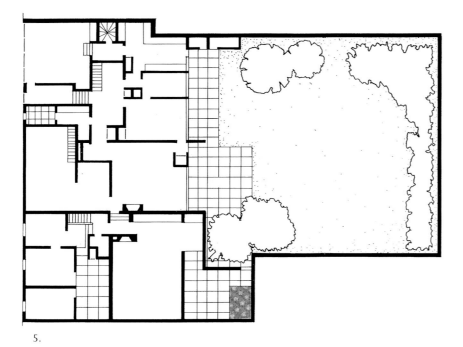

5.

Barragán worked back from his initial preoccupation with the overall topography to the design of individual dwellings. This trajectory reached its apotheosis in his Folke Egerstrom House, completed at San

Cristobal, Mexico City, in 1968. Around an all but anonymous International Style house, Barragán gave pride of place to a horse yard, a water fountain, and a pond that occupied the center of the entire composition. The pink and red walls of the corral and the stables that pinwheel around the pond demonstrate the peculiar admixture of vernacular form and modern abstraction that was to become the touchstone of Barragán's style. The deeper critical ethos of his work, however, lies embodied in his aphorism: "All architecture which does not express serenity fails in its spiritual mission. Thus it has been a mistake to abandon the shelter of walls for the inclemency of large areas of glass."[3]

Legorreta began where Barragán left off, first in the Hotel Camino Real in Mexico City in 1968, and then in a number of monopitched houses of the early 1970s. Preoccupied with large commissions for the next decade and a half, he did not return to domestic building until the mid-1980s, first in the Casa Montalban, built in the Hollywood Hills for the Mexican actor Ricardo Montalban in 1985, and then in the Greenberg House, completed in Los Angeles in 1991. These houses employ the same basic syntax: high, blocky masonry masses and walls roughly rendered in earth-colored plaster, with the occasional plane accented in bright color. Built according to habitually generous Mexican space standards, these works convey a sense of luxury totally foreign to the North American scene. Large outriding courts, subtle changes in level, grilled screens, reflecting pools, and carefully framed panoramas further enhance the overall sense of hedonistic calm.

Mark Mack and Andrew Batey turned to this Mexican minimalist, late modern vernacular in the 1970s when they formed their partnership in San Francisco. In 1978 they completed their Anti-Villa (fig. 6), the first in a series of neo-primitive houses realized in the Napa Valley. These villas were often conceived, in conjunction with vineyards, as directly serving the local viticulture. Made of exposed fair-face concrete block and half buried into the slope of a wooded site, the initial Mack and Batey Anti-Villa did not aspire to some kind of picturesque rusticity. Instead, modern materials and methods were employed to recall the tradition of the Palladian villa in a totally fresh way. Thus concrete block and standard steel sash were used to contrast with a wooden pergola that was intended both to carry grapes and to function as a sun shade. In 1982 the architects wrote of its intent in the following terms:

6.

. . . [The neo-primitive] is conservative in its reaching back to a well-mastered building technology, progressive in promoting a utopian purism, intellectual in its reduction of architectural principles, and emotional in its rugged natural form tied to its site condition.

The insubstantial artificial building materials which have produced the post-modern aesthetic suits the confused language of lowered expectations and applied ornament. This has increased the distance between the natural environment and the built artifact. The structural vernacular combined with the desire to fit the building into the landscape reinforces the notion of permanence, and counters the vicissitudes of fleeting trendiness now rampant in architecture . . .

It is the ruins of Pompeii, the classicism of Schinkel and Asplund, the archetypal austerity of Loos and Barragán, rather than Las Vegas, that inspire us.[4]

While the Batey-Mack partnership was relatively short lived, Mack has since gone on to practice under his own name, first in San Francisco and more recently in Los Angeles. Although he has since modified the austerity and symmetry of his early concrete-block aesthetic, he nonetheless remains faithful to many of the neo-primitivist tenets, emphasizing the sociocultural significance of program, the need to integrate the house into the site, and the overriding importance of tectonic expression in architectural form.

An unusual affinity has prevailed between Mack's work and that of Steven Holl. This mutual influence is particularly evident in Holl's unrealized Metz House, designed for Staten Island, New York, in 1980. Holl used similar code, namely naked concrete block in simple prismatic shapes, to meet the very different demands of a sculptor and a painter. The house excluded conventional living and dining rooms in favor of two large studios and a large common kitchen. The categorically different studios were supposed to reflect the contrasting sensibilities of the artistic couple. Overall, the house generated a dialectic of two segments around a traditional U-shaped courtyard.

Ten projects later, Holl would finally realize one of his typological paradigms in the Berkowitz House, built on Martha's Vineyard in 1984. Aside from meeting the basic demands of a vacation house, the Berkowitz House characteristically synthesizes the mythic and the typological. Here the myth is drawn from Herman Melville's *Moby-Dick*. As Holl puts it: "According to Melville's *Moby-Dick*, the Indian tribe that originally inhabited Martha's Vineyard created a unique dwelling type. Finding a whale skeleton on the beach, they would pull it up to dry land and stretch skins and bark over it, transforming it into a house."[5]

Thus the Berkowitz House brings myth and type together in an inside-out balloon frame evoking both the profile of a ship and a mammal's skeleton. Without directly alluding to nautical form, this long, single-story house terminates in a two-story tower at one end that unavoidably recalls a ship's wheelhouse. Readable as a ruined vessel, the exposed four-by-six framework of the house also suggests the skeleton of a primitive hut. On sunny days the chinoiserie of the timber balustrade casts a decorative shadow over the body of the building. Although the house steps down the slope, it is suspended above the dunes along its entire length. Holl imposed completely different expressions on the landward and seaward sides of the house; the former featuring an entry via a granite step, the latter being crowned by a sun deck and an open timber pergola facing the ocean.

Holl's feeling for such oppositions, replete with symbolic and cultural associations, finds further expression here in the interior lighting, above in the prowlike belvedere facing west and in the triangular, peaked, plate-glass skylight over the kitchen. Holl's obsession with achieving rich material effects through the internal finishes first announces itself in the Berkowitz House but will be further elaborated in a number of interiors that he designed around this time; first the

Cohen Apartment, New York, of 1984 (fig. 7) and second the Giada Showroom, New York, of 1987, both of which employed lacquer surfaces and sand-blasted cast glass.

Equally rich surfaces characterize the domestic work of the Chicago architect Ronald Krueck, who, in collaboration with Keith Olsen, realized an exceptionally compact, if large, courtyard house on North Larrabie Street, Chicago, in 1980. Educated at Mies van der Rohe's Illinois Institute of Technology, Krueck reinterpreted Mies in terms of Charles Eames on one hand and Pierre Chareau on the other. The

7.

skeletonal, modular precision of this house points in two directions at once, first to the California Case Study houses and second to Chareau's canonical Maison deVerre, built in Paris in 1932.

From the early 1980s onward the American modern house began to assume different expressions in different parts of the country, so that it became virtually impossible to identify any particular trend or trends as being peculiarly American. A widespread antimodernism assumed a variety of forms in domestic architecture, ranging from Michael Graves's toylike neoclassicism to Robert Stern's cannibal- ization of the American colonial tradition, not to mention Andreas Duany and Elizabeth Plater-Zyberk's southern variation on equally reactionary historicist themes in their extensive Florida practice. Here and there, the equally nostalgic trope of the jazz moderne announced itself, above all in Arquitectonica's Spear House, designed by Laurinda Spear and Bernardo Fort-Brescia for her parents in 1978. A more austere allusion to the same genre appears in the Schreyer House by Jennings and Stout, completed after a long gestation period in Healdsburg, California, in 1990. This work deftly recalls the Cubistic architecture of Rob-Mallet Stevens, as this first appeared in Paris in the second half of the 1920s. Both houses have in common an equally

164

hedonistic approach to form and color that recalls the work of Antoine Predock, although Predock's work is more earthbound.

In the same decade two other manifestations appeared with sufficient consistency as to constitute an explicit continuation of earlier lines. First is the work of the latter-day Southern California School, particu- larly evident in the 1970s and the early 1980s in the work of Helmut Schulitz and Peter de Bretteville, both of whom built remarkable, "off-the-peg" high-tech houses in the Beverly Hills and Laurel Canyon districts of Los Angeles. As rigorous as anything previously achieved by John Entenza's Case Study houses, these works insist on the still- untapped potential of prefabricated form. Something of this potential turned up more recently in the twenty-by-seventy-five-foot live/ work loft built in downtown San Francisco in 1991 to the designs of Richard Stacy of the firm of Tanner, Leddy, Maytum. Something similar may be claimed for Smith-Miller and Hawkinson's revamping of a late neo-Neutra house erected in Beverly Hills by Donald Polsky in the early 1960s. Ironically, this 1991 effort led Smith-Miller and Hawkinson to create a dynamic, hi-tech assembly closer to the spirit of Polsky's Austrian master than to his own much more revisionist modern manner.

At the same time it is still possible to find, here and there, a continu- ation of Wright's Prairie Style, which seems to remain plausible as a modus operandi. Nowhere is this more evident than in the romantic work of Fay Jones. Jones's finest neo-Wrightian residence to date remains the L-shaped house that he built in Bentonville, Arkansas, in 1962. With its long, shallow pitched roof finished in cedar shingles, paralleled by an equally long glass canopy that reinforces this line as it spans a stream, this house evokes the entire trajectory of Wright's career from his first Taliesin house built in 1914 to Fallingwater realized in 1936. No one has captured the essential spirit of the Bentonville House better than Frank Israel, who wrote in 1978:

...The low horizontal structure, roughly L-shaped, was built of local Arkansas fieldstone on a bluff that had a stream running along the base. The architect dammed up the stream in order to create a pond that reflects a view of the house, and a waterfall that echoes a harmonious relationship between the man-made and the natural. The long main section of the house borders the pond and waterfall; the short game-room wing bridges the flowing stream, as architecture and landscape merge into a single composition.

. . . The house is open to the west, overlooking the water. A continuous wall of glass, broken only by a series of flagstone piers, provides each interior space of this one-level open plan with an

expansive view. The view shows water as a procession: a flat, placid pond becomes a lively waterfall, then returns to its original form, a stream. An outdoor walkway follows this side of the house, linking the inside and outside. It is contained by a thin delicate railing of red cedar.[6]

An equally romantic output, generating a totally different environment, occurs in the remarkable output of William Bruder, working out of Phoenix, Arizona. Like Fay Jones, Bruder is indebted to the legacy of Wright, only here the line of inspiration passes as much through Bruce Goff as through Wright himself.

Unlike Goff, however, Bruder refuses to allow his ad hoc approach to

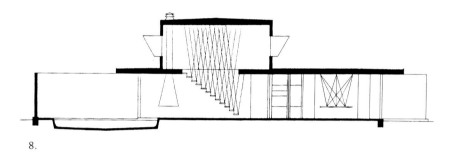

8.

Galvanized metal, sandblasted concrete block, and rusted steel joists have been part of his oeuvre for 15 years, as have standard aluminum frames modified into pivot-swing doors, like the one at the Murray residence.

Bruder's experience as a sculptor undoubtedly fostered his hands-on approach with mundane materials; perhaps his preference for unpointed materials likewise originated in the art studio . . . as in most of his structures, color is integral to the building materials—from the aggregate of the roof, which matches the color of the earth, to the red particles mixed into the concrete aggregate of the masonry walls, and the pale tone of the maple cabinetry inside . . .

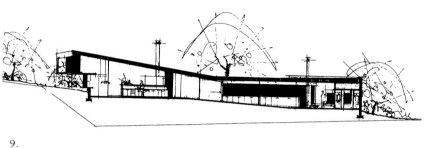

9.

veer into kitsch. Instead he maintains a certain vitality and aesthetic rigor through his mastery of completely different modern traditions, some of them being of Nordic origin. Bruder's work recalls figures as diverse as Alvar Aalto in his 1975 Credit Union, Phoenix, or Sverre Fehn in his own house built in the desert during the same year. The Korach House of 1975 further recalls both Aalto and Hugo Haring. More local influences are Paul Schweiker and the Swiss emigré Albert Frey, who has practiced for years in nearby Palm Springs. Frey's own house (fig. 8), under development from 1947 to 1953, lies significantly close to the work of Bruder.

A key aspect of Bruder's work in the desert is his concern for designing houses that are environmentally and ecologically effective; hence the evaporative cooling unit with exposed ducts incorporated into the design of his own house. Bruder has built more than forty houses in seventeen years, and his hands-on, Schindler-like approach to both construction and materials has enabled him to build inexpensive houses of exceptional freshness and vitality. A typical example is his Murray House (fig. 9) built in the Sonoran Desert in Arizona in 1990. Of this achievement Philip Arcidi wrote:

The reflective metal cladding on the broad hood was the dividend of a budget cut. Bruder's drawings originally specified copper, but the cheaper galvanized surface is more brilliant, and its corrugated surface accentuates the incline of the roof. . . .[7]

Despite the acute angled geometry of its plan the Murray House could not be further from the paradoxically "deconstructivist" aestheticism that informs the work of the Los Angeles architect Thom Mayne of Morphosis or that of Mack Scogin and Merrill Elam, a husband-and-wife team, practicing out of Atlanta. In both instances, constructional-cum-spatial pyrotechnics seem to arise more out of aesthetic and formal preconceptions than out of finding an appropriate pragmatic and poetic response to the requirements of the brief.

Such deconstructivist works as Mayne's Crawford House of 1991 (fig. 10, page 166) and Scogin Elam and Bray's Chmar House of 1990 evidently relate to the equally aformal-formal domestic work of Southern Californian architect Frank Gehry, beginning with Gehry's own "deconstructed" suburban house, which he partially demolished and then expanded in Los Angeles in 1979. Close to his California colleagues Mayne and Eric Owen Moss, Gehry could hardly be further removed from the reserved modernism of W. G. Clark of Charleston or the neo-purism of Anthony Ames practicing in Atlanta.

Ames's white, neo-rationalist houses dating from the mid-1970s are altogether more formal and severe than Clark's own brand of neo-primitivism, as this may be found in his Reid House built on Johns Island, South Carolina, in 1976.

Looking back over the spectrum of American domestic building throughout the century, one notices that the center of creative energy has moved inexorably westward. The innovative spirit of the Shingle Style that emerged with such vigor on the East Coast in the last two decades of the nineteenth century had already shifted to Chicago by the the turn of the century. This creative impulse emerged as the so-called Prairie Style over the next decade and a half and then it moved on to the West Coast and the Southwest where it seems to have remained ever since. Western and Southwestern architects and, more importantly, their clients seem to emerge from the sunbelt as perennially adventuresome personalities, ever ready to commit the design of their homes to relatively untried talent. Today this factor would seem to be more crucial than ever, particularly in the United States where, given the increasing absence of the public client, the domestic realm is the only area in which the country's architectural culture can remain alive.

As I have already intimated in the introduction, it was just as difficult to choose houses from the production of the last two decades as it had been to select from the output of the previous ninety years. Herein, perhaps more than before, we have extended the rubric of a masterwork to include some relatively modest houses not only in terms of their size but also for the way in which the format of the dwelling had been formulated in each instance. Thus we opted for two somewhat offbeat works: for a small country house on the shores of Ballston Lake in upper New York State and for a town house in the Ukrainian Village in downtown Chicago. Apart from their intrinsic quality a salient factor in both instances was their unusual manner of construction and the overall effect this has had on their general character. In the first case the constitution of the building out of very large precast concrete wall panels; in the second, the facing of the house in precision, fair-faced brickwork with matching mortar—both modes being rather atypical for domestic building in the United States today and yet both being seemingly appropriate to the context in which they are situated.

166

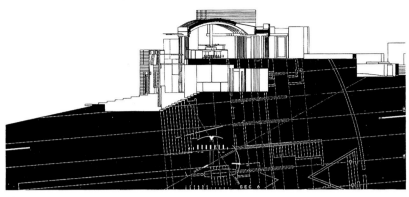

10.

We have also included the residence and studio of the architect Carlos Jiménez for all the mutations this diminutive complex has been through over the last quarter century. Apart from being a unique example of progressive suburban development in downtown Houston, this house and studio is of interest because of the way in which it reveals the fundamental interchangeability of the two units— the way in which one is inseparable from the other, just as Jiménez hardly discriminates between the process of living and the act of creating.

As to the remaining houses included in this edition, they represent a fairly wide spectrum of high-end luxury accommodation. In almost every instance, like Richard Neutra's Kaufmann House in the desert of 1946, they also entail a precisely inflected relationship to the landscape in which they are situated.

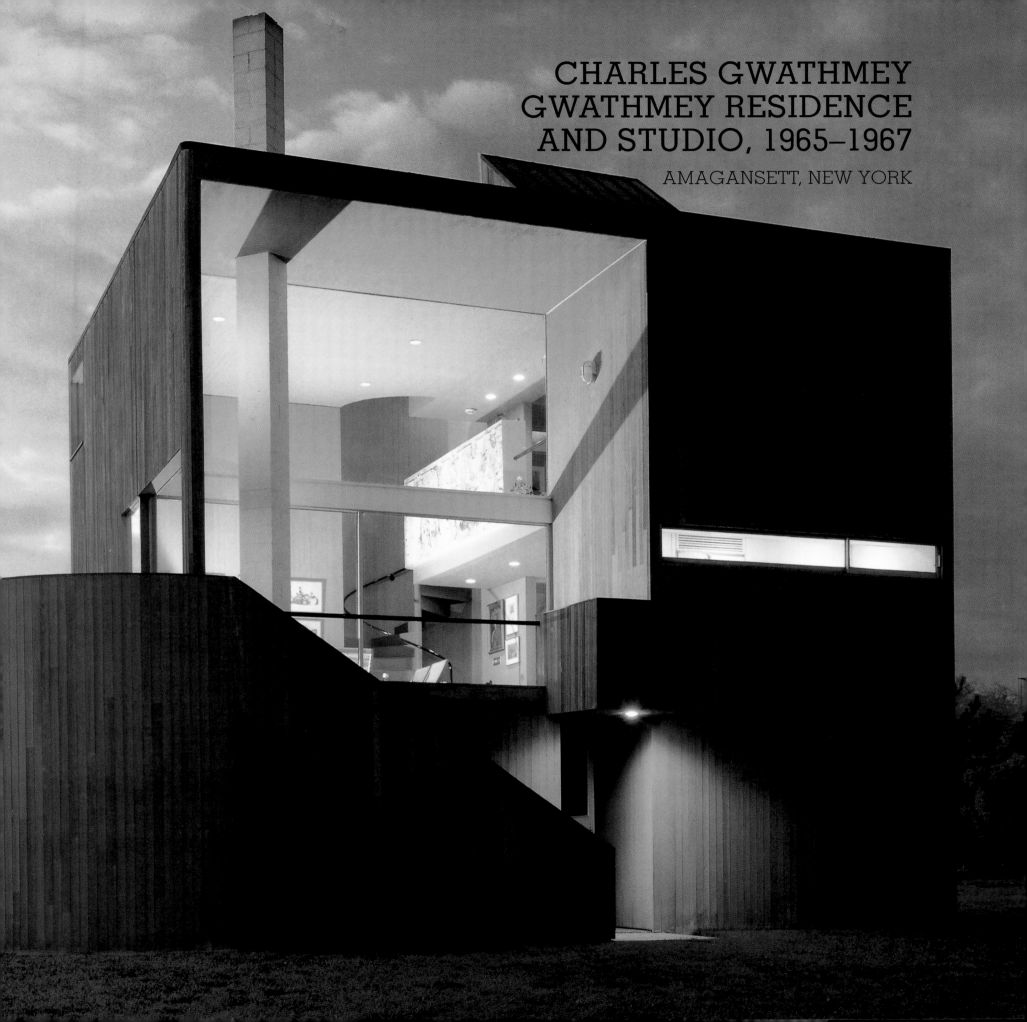

CHARLES GWATHMEY
GWATHMEY RESIDENCE
AND STUDIO, 1965–1967

AMAGANSETT, NEW YORK

This complex, built for the architect's parents, consists of a house and a studio, each identically finished in tongue-and-groove cedar siding. The two freestanding cubic elements rotate about each other in such a way that there is no one viewpoint from which they may be ideally perceived. Thus, the composition constantly changes from the initial sweeping entry of the car to a more measured pedestrian approach along a narrow walkway set at forty-five degrees to the main house.

This interplay also turns upon mutual secondary forms such as the copper-clad, monopitched roofs to the skylights of the house and the studio; the dialectic between countervailing pitches, facing northeast and north, is further reinforced by other components,

such as the exposed cylindrical and semicircular stairs and a large recessed balcony on the second floor of the house.

While the house is a three-bedroom dwelling, the two-story studio is also treated as a living unit with guest bedroom and bathroom at grade and a studio above. The public and private functions of the house are stacked vertically, with the bedrooms and the study located on the first floor and the living, dining, kitchen en suite on the second. Overlooking the living room, the upstand of the master bedroom is decorated with an enlarged photo-reproduction of a Mesopotamian wall relief, a conceit seemingly inspired by the antique plaster casts that Paul Rudolph applied to the walls of the Art and Architecture Building at Yale University.

The overall character of the internal space is inflected by a series of unique details including a freestanding concrete-block chimney set on the diagonal, a continuous strip window to the dining area, and the turning of the last treads of the spiral stair into the living room so as to invite entry. These devices plus a material palette comprising redwood decking, birch-veneered cabinetwork, and aluminum-framed

fenestration are brought together here for the first time as
the quintessential Gwathmey manner.

Derived from Marcel Breuer and from the domestic architecture of
Edward Larrabee Barnes, with whom Gwathmey served a short
apprenticeship, this syntax is overlaid with Purist tropes drawn from
the work of Le Corbusier. Linked through its boarded skin to the

domestic tradition of the East Coast and distanced from the "white"
avant-gardism of the International Style, this house is thus a modern
reinterpretation of Shingle-Style values. Over the next decade the
architect elaborated this language in one beautifully crafted residence
after another, beginning with the Straus House, in Purchase, New
York, of 1968, and culminating, at least as a discernible series, in the
Charof Residence, completed in Montauk, New York, in 1976.

LOUIS KAHN
KORMAN HOUSE, 1971–1973

FORT WASHINGTON, PENNSYLVANIA

The private house was always an awkward subject for Kahn; he seems invariably to have vascillated between treating it as a free form and handling it as a diminutive institutional structure, with all the formal propriety that this demands. The Fisher House of 1960 exemplifies the first approach while the second is best represented by the unbuilt Morris House designed for Mount Kisco, New York, in 1958. It may be argued Kahn only attained a balance between these countervailing approaches in two houses: the unbuilt Adler House dating from 1954 and the Korman House, begun in 1972 and finished just prior to his death.

The grandeur of this house is established from the outset by its site— seventy acres of relatively unspoilt meadowland, replete with large deciduous trees and bounded on all sides by wooden fences and horse farms. The intimate link established between the site and the biaxial plan of the house is essential to the poetry of the work. To this end, large plate-glass windows frame views of the landscape at every turn as one passes from one room to the next.

174

Built to meet the needs of a gregarious family of six—a couple and their four sons—the rooms of the Korman House are grouped around an open stair hall of generous proportions served by a monumental freestanding wooden stair. Supported by nine square posts and fleshed out with planks and oak railings, this stair recalls the companionway of a ship. A second, equally heavy timber stair winds up the center of the house, linking the first-floor master bedroom to the den. These monumental masterpieces in structural fir are matched by the one-inch oak planking used throughout for the floor and walls, up to the first story.

In this final house Kahn maintained his all but mythical balance between "served" and "servant" elements through the internal articulation of the stairs and the external expression of the service cores. Four timber-framed bathrooms are set back-to-back across the axis of the boys' wing together with three brick chimney shafts, the pinwheeling location of which contrasts with the four-square format house, recalling, albeit distantly, the symmetrically paired chimneys of Stratford Hall in Virginia. This reference is reinforced by the monumental living room elevation, with its twelve square plate-glass windows. Two chimneys terminate this facade, suggesting the asymmetrical/symmetrical counterpoint of the rest of the house by emerging from the timber frame at slightly different heights.

Kahn carried this asymmetrical/symmetrical play further in the master bedroom and roof deck situated behind the southeastern stack. He had originally intended to complement this provision with wooden shutters set into the wall separating the master bedroom from the upper part of the living room, but the client regrettably resisted this relationship and effect.

Devices of this order had a particular significance for Kahn, since they enabled him to think of each building as a large piece of cabinetwork. This conceit is evident in the Korman House in Kahn's insistence on panelling segments of the external membrane as opposed to the vertical cypress siding that in the main is used throughout.

Despite its biaxial plan, the house constantly changes as one moves around it, and this asymmetry combined with a stand of pine trees planted at the time of its completion, serves to integrate its rather severe form into the slightly undulating ground.

The vertical, boarded cladding and flush timber trim give the house a taut membranous quality that is in strong contrast to the heavy brick

chimneys that rise out of the brick-paved terraces that surround the house and extend into the kitchen and breakfast room. Built of the same material, each fireplace is covered by a rubbed-brick arch while the principal hearth in the living room is flanked by an inglenook.

In its use of materials, the Korman House, like all of Kahn's houses, is a convincing attempt to evoke the existential purity of Shaker culture.

RICHARD MEIER
DOUGLAS HOUSE, 1971–1973

HARBOR SPRINGS, MICHIGAN

The Douglas House is situated on a precipitous cliff overlooking Lake Michigan and is shielded on all sides by a cover of conifers. The densely forested character of the site gives the impression that the house has been dropped into position by helicopter. This pristine object stands poised above the natural world, creating a sharp contrast between the whiteness of its form and the color of the water, the landscape, and the sky. The exterior is clad in glass and flush vertical wood siding. All surfaces except the floor have been painted white, emphasizing the lightweight character of the balloon-frame wall, and this dematerialization becomes even more extreme in the three sides of the belvedere living room facing the lake, which are clad in large sheets of plate glass.

The Douglas House closely relates to Meier's Smith House, built in Darien, Connecticut, in 1967; the clients demanded an all but identical house for a very different site. In both houses, however, Meier treats the entry as a passerelle running back beyond the building into the wooden landscape. In the Douglas House the steep grade necessitated entering the house via a footbridge situated at roof level. Thus, from the landward side only the roof and top floor are visible, and only when one crosses the bridge does one become aware of the full five stories of the house descending below. A second bridge directly below provides access to the lower slope and, ultimately, via a stair, a catwalk, and a ladder, to the beach.

185

The entry foyer gives on to the living and dining levels below and out to the roof deck overlooking the lake. As in the Smith House, the semi-public and private spaces are expressed by solid and glazed walls, respectively.

The western, semi-public face opens toward the lake from all floors.
On the eastern side, facing the road, a solid wall with small windows
shields the private zone containing bedrooms and services on three
floors. The curved skylight on the roof deck illuminates the center
of the house, with light falling down into the dining level two
floors below. This zenithal light unifies all the levels, and its location
reinforces a shear line separating the public and private sectors.

188

Unlike the Smith House, horizontal corridors, open to the view, offer some interplay between the public and private parts of the house, between the openness of the living area and the closed character of the bedrooms. The corridor wall is pierced by horizontal windows that not only open to the rear of the house but also admit light coming in from above.

On the upper level a landing, projecting over the double-height living volume, serves as a study. Diagonally opposite the main stair, linking all levels, is a second external steel stair connecting the bedrooms to the main living floor and beyond this, via a cantilevered stair, to the lakefront below.

The fireplace is one of the most significant statements in the house and the chimney, prominently situated in the midst of the western elevation, competes for attention with the lake panorama that surrounds it. This nostalgic gesture to the memory of the hearth, set at the very limit of this vitreous and pristine house, could hardly be more removed from Wright's concept of the fire burning deep in the heart of the prairie house.

192

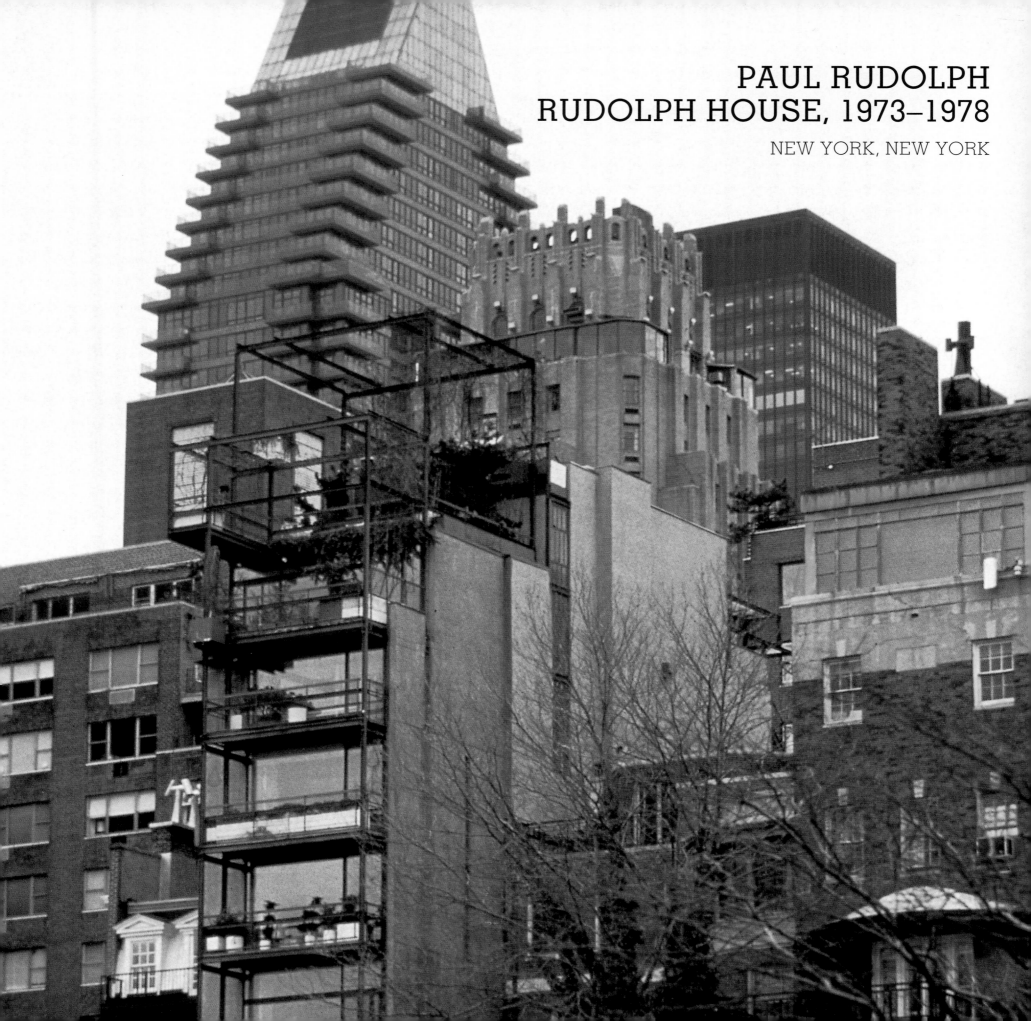

PAUL RUDOLPH
RUDOLPH HOUSE, 1973–1978

NEW YORK, NEW YORK

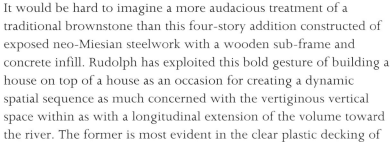

It would be hard to imagine a more audacious treatment of a traditional brownstone than this four-story addition constructed of exposed neo-Miesian steelwork with a wooden sub-frame and concrete infill. Rudolph has exploited this bold gesture of building a house on top of a house as an occasion for creating a dynamic spatial sequence as much concerned with the vertiginous vertical space within as with a longitudinal extension of the volume toward the river. The former is most evident in the clear plastic decking of the footbridges that connect the riserless staircase running throughout the section to serve the various levels that articulate the internal volume. At the same time, the vertical displacement in space is touched with a playful voyeurism as we may judge from the transparent jacuzzi and sink in the main bathroom opening to the spaces below. The same sink, when artificially lit, is intended to function as an internal fountain compounded of light and water.

This rather theatrical preoccupation with transparency and glistening light effects is reinforced by applying raw silk to the walls and by covering almost every exposed structural member with silver laminate. The metallic effect is echoed by an ingenious steel plate linking the main sitting room with the bedroom. Throughout the house, this brilliance is offset by continuous low-level seating upholstered in either black leather or beige velvet. The floors where not transparent are covered in gray carpet.

Despite these intriguing, partly cavernous, Soanesque effects, this house assumes a sublime aspect as it extends out toward a

196

suspended terrace overlooking the river. Flanked by vertically fenestrated, continuous glazing on its southern elevation, the building becomes more unequivocally tectonic as it breaks out toward the water. With some justification Rudolph regards this spectacular view of the East River as having aristocratic dimensions, particularly on the Fourth of July when, as he puts it, Macy's annual fireworks display makes one feel like Louis XIV.

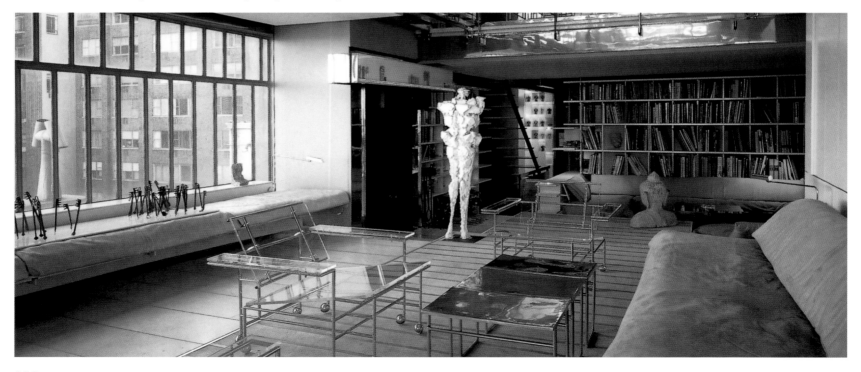

PETER DE BRETTEVILLE
WILLOW GLEN HOUSES, 1973–1975

LOS ANGELES, CALIFORNIA

This double house, initially built for two separate families who were active in the arts, has certain obvious precedents in the architecture of Southern California, above all, perhaps, the double courtyard house built by Schindler for himself and Clive Chase in 1923 and the house and studio that Charles and Ray Eames built in Pacific Palisades in 1949. However, the strictly modular lightweight constructional system employed by De Bretteville is somewhat at variance with both of these houses. This double-fronted building is cut into the steep slope of a half-acre canyon site that is accessed along its lower edge. The initial excavation provided for automobile access, garages, and workshop space along this frontage.

This arrangement yielded a largely blank, three-story frontal elevation covered in vertical corrugated sheeting, with cutout apertures to provide light and limited access to the workspaces on the ground floor.

201

The two houses read as a continuous form along this frontage, where a central blank panel is framed by a pair of stairways giving access to the upper garden side of the complex. These stairs double back to feed a common balcony overlooking the street. On the two-story, western garden facade, the modular framework of the house is either left open or filled with glass.

Predicated throughout on a four-foot module and a four-by-four-foot cube, these houses are organized around an eight-by-twenty-eight-foot structural bay. Square tubular-steel columns carry a concrete slab on the first floor and truss joists at the roof; exposed two-by-four-inch rafters, carried on joist hangers, are let into the top chord of the truss joists. These joists are also made up of two-by-fours for the top and bottom chords with latticework steel tubing in between.

Unlike the prototypical Eames House, where the module is much smaller and thus open to a wider range of all but painterly manipulation, the architect has insisted here on maintaining his four-by-four-foot module, so that all side-hung doors and top-hung windows conform to the same overriding square grid. The grid is relieved by a four-foot-deep outriding pipe-rail trellis, with detachable canvas awnings, on the garden side. This shield against horizontal light is suspended from a cantilevered second-floor balcony, the floor of which is covered in boiler plate, open decking. Similar steel decking is applied to the same plane on the opposite side of the house to allow top light to penetrate to the lower levels.

202

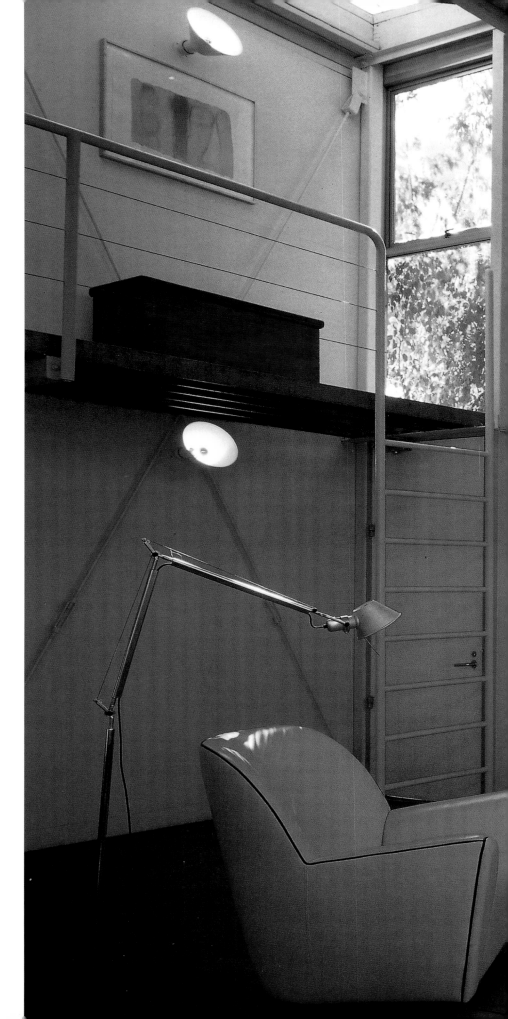

Each house is furnished differently despite the fact that it is made of the same modular system. As Peter Papademetriou has written:

Aside from the conceptual schematic differences between the projects, the furnishing of each house by the particular families has yielded nearly completely different environments. The de Brettevilles felt that an auto body shop actually suited their needs, were informed on the warehouse idea, and particularly like hardware items. Consequently, their house is essentially white on the interior, including all wood items; counters and cabinets are white plastic laminate, rubber stud tile floors in wet areas are black. Color is not used systematically to "explain" relationships (as in Schulitz) but in a subtle manner. The core walls are slightly gray, steel beams are yellow, there is a pink staircase and doors are chalkboard-green. The industrial design effect is completed by the concrete floor, sealed to a rusty color. Where certain standard items didn't suit the design, de Bretteville designed his own, such as the improvised "Brion Vega" grilles for forced air registers.

Like the almost contemporaneous Helmut Schulitz houses built in Beverly Hills, the double-fronted De Bretteville/Simon house represents a swansong, so to speak, in the West Coast tradition of rational, modular building production dating back to the pioneering work of Neutra, Eames, Ellwood, and Soriano.

In the Simon house, all steel was left shop-primed, the truss and wooden roof were left natural. Rubber studded tile is rust color, all countertops in the kitchen are butcher block, and cabinet surfaces are a natural wood veneer. Interior core walls are painted a peach color, with buff-tan on the lower portion. The Simons' house is as warm and soft as the de Brettevilles' is cool. Combining this warm and soft scheme with a more conventional arrangement of parts, the Simon house probably answers most people's definition of what a home might be.

206

PETER EISENMAN
HOUSE VI, 1972–1976

WEST CORNWALL, CONNECTICUT

It is fitting that this house was completed just before the publication of Charles Jencks's influential survey, *The Language of Post-Modern Architecture* (1977) for if anything presaged the advent of postmodernism it is surely the Frank House, numbered by the architect as part of a didactic series. Coming into being after nearly four decades of the functionalist modern movement, when the ideas of the European avant-garde were disseminated in the United States, House VI was part of an effort to bring this tradition to closure by self-consciously departing from the socially ameliorative and liberative promise of the original movement toward a more formal, post-humanist attitude.

In this regard House VI participates in the postmodernist ethos since there is little evidence here of the utopian thrust that is still implicit in the late New Deal work of certain European emigrés. One thinks in particular of the early partnership of Walter Gropius and Marcel Breuer or of the later collaboration between Serge Chermayeff and Christopher Alexander. This utopian line begins to lose its conviction in the 1960s, at least in part due to the neo-cubist aestheticism of the so-called New York Five, of which Eisenman was a prime mover.

In certain respects House VI may be seen as an extremely subtle reinterpretation and synthesis of the work of two seminal avant-garde architects of the prewar period: the Dutch De Stijl architect Gerrit Rietveld and Italian Rationalist Giuseppe Terragni. One particular work by Terragni haunted Eisenman throughout his early career, namely, the Giuliani Frigerio apartments completed on the shores of Lake Como in 1939–40.

House VI emerges out of a fusion between two equally radical yet somewhat antithetical concepts; on the one hand Terragni's preoccupation with layered-rotational space, lying just behind the outer face of the building, and on the other Rietveld's ultimate exercise in centrifugal composition, his canonical Rietveld-Schroeder House built in Utrecht in 1924. House VI appears as an amalgamation of the two concepts in that the stair hall of the Giuliani Frigerio block is condensed, so to speak, into the cross-axial plane of House VI. This aspatial planar gesture denies, as it were, the core of spiraling space, taken from the Rietveld-Schroeder House, that would otherwise account for the pinwheeling dispersal of its elements around the periphery of House VI.

Axonometric showing wall notation and counterpoint between the stairs.

210

Aside from this deliberate conceptual disjunction, House VI asserts itself as a minimalist work that, like the artworks of Sol Lewitt, Donald Judd, Ad Reinhardt, and Barnett Newman, insists on its own factual formal autonomy, renouncing the potentially expressive figuration of functionalist form. Yet while Eisenman systematically denied the utopian promise of the International Style architecture of the 1930s, he was equally distanced from the theosophic modernism of painters

like Piet Mondrian and Kasimir Malevich. The cosmogonic, primary colors of Dr. Schoenmaeker's Christosophy have been replaced in House VI by indexically coded green and red stairs, the former serving quite literally to connect the floors of the house, the latter being a mirror image suspended over the dining hall as an inaccessible, Escher-like anti-stair.

Eisenman writes of this inversion with all the syntactic rigor of a serial musician unwilling to make pragmatic concessions to Norbet Weiner's "human use of human beings," a view that still prevailed in the 1960s as an ameliorative aspiration. In the mid-1970s Eisenman wrote of turning the space of his houses inside out and of thus beginning the experiential narrative of the concept from the center outward. This is the ostensible rationale for painting the interior of House VI white and the exterior gray, implying that one is outside when one is inside and inside when one is outside. In this way the house is elaborately color-coded so that one may perceive the white cruciform planar elements of the interior penetrating to the exterior and so on. Experientially, the building is as much about "absences" as "presences" with vertical, floor-to-ceiling windows and interior slots standing for absent walls and vice versa.

This dichotomous prescription favors the axonometric projection adopted by the prewar avant-garde, a form of projection that conveniently allows one to distance oneself from the spatial experience of the object. Through this heuristic device combining both the orthogonal and the diagonal projection, Eisenman sustained the process of binomial subdivision that appears to have determined the formal order of the house. Hence the provision of glass slots in the walls, floors, and ceilings, which create a kind of virtual architecture, a desiccated house within a house, unparalleled in contemporary production except perhaps in the metamorphological approach of the Japanese architect Hiromi Fujii.

Perhaps in no other building has Eisenman arrived at such a dense orchestration of impacted form, comprised simultaneously of precisely interrelated planes, transparencies, volumes, and masses. In this sense the work is unique and deserves to be ranked with the equally canonical works from which it derives its inspiration and possibly with other pioneering minimalist pieces of a very different genre, such as Mies van der Rohe's Farnsworth House of 1951.

MICHAEL GRAVES
GRAVES HOUSE, 1977–1993

PRINCETON, NEW JERSEY

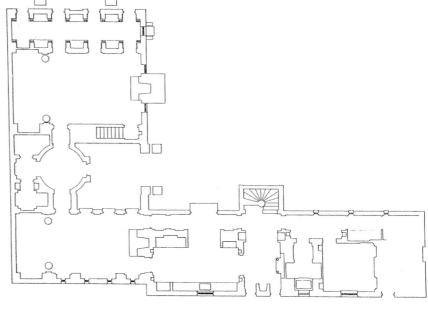

Situated on the outer limits of a university town and isolated on a back lot between a small public park and a side street, this warehouse building dating from the mid-1920s has now been transformed into a romantic residence. Since Graves purchased the hollow terra-cotta block and brick shell in 1972, the structure has been through two incarnations. Little of the initial conversion now remains save for a secondary bathroom that is more decorative in tone than the Gandyesque taste that prevails in the rest of the house.

Rendered in a purplish-beige stucco and looking in many ways like a Belgian "moderne" work of the mid-1920s this two-story house with its forecourt and drive divides into two sections: a public wing facing the forecourt and a private wing running parallel to the main approach, which is lined with poplars on both sides. The east and west forecourts are enclosed by fences, painted dark gray and viridian. One may enter the property by car along a drive approaching from a side street to the south or on foot through a public park to the east. Except for the lawn in the forecourt in front of the library, the house is surrounded by rice-stone gravel that conveys a peculiarly Gallic feeling.

216

The entrance to the house is through a shallow pergola and a diminutive square court graced by the sound of water cascading into an antique basin. The entry hall itself is a rotunda lit from above by an oculus passing through the full height of the house. This space leads into a sequence of carefully modulated neoclassical rooms culminating at the eastern end in a low, squarish sitting room and top-lit library facing the lawn and at the opposite end in a narrow dining hall lit by gridded windows.

As in Sir John Soane's house, realized in London some one hundred and fifty years ago, this house comprises an enfilade of axially related chambers and aedicules of varying size. A layer of vaulted spaces runs along the northern wall, providing shallow alcoves at the end of the sitting and dining spaces, each bracketed by short Tuscan columns.

Behind each column are narrow clerestories set into the upper part of the vault. These provide a modicum of natural light in what would otherwise be rather dark spaces.

In contrast, the library is brightly lit by a skylight running its full length, and the sitting room by the tall windows set to either side of the chimney breast.

Aside from the dining room and kitchen, the private wing contains a series of ancillary spaces including a narrow breakfast room that, like the library, is lit from above. This extremely compact space, with built-in storage and display shelves, is graced by a small fireplace and chimney breast faced in white glazed Paris Metro tiles. Gridded, glazed full-height steel doors on either side lead out to the rear court, making it one of the most intimate rooms of the house.

This space is located on the axis of a winding stair that leads up to the three-bedroom, three-bathroom sequence above plus the upper parts of ground-floor volumes—the breakfast room, rotunda, and library— that are now capped by skylights.

222

Delicately lit, with ceiling spots and sconces designed by the architect (among Graves's most brilliant designs are those for light fittings), the Warehouse, as it is fondly called, is indeed a house of wares since, above all, as with Soane, it is the house of a collector. Paradoxical as it may seem, Graves's taste remains transfixed on the same epoch; hence the Biedermeier furniture, the antique plaster casts and occasional bronze or alabaster sculpture, and the gold-framed wallpaper drawn from a German villa. All of this is leavened by the more catholic contents of the library, by Viennese side chairs from the turn of the century, richly upholstered in velvet, and throughout the house, and gridded, somewhat Hoffmanesque fenestration painted veridian.

Even in this land of boundless private opulence, one would be hard pressed to find a house where the cult of *Selbstbildung* has been taken to such an extreme. Yet despite such introspective aestheticism the Warehouse remains intimate, generous, and, above all, calm.

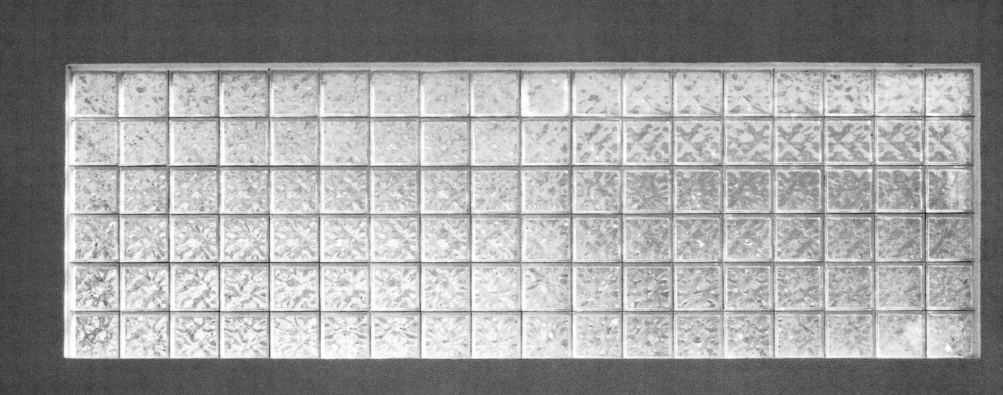

Following an initial sketch made by Laurinda Spear and Rem Koolhaas, this house is one of the first projects of Arquitectonica. The newly formed firm then comprised Hervin Romney, Andreas Duany, Elizabeth Plater-Zyberk, Bernardo Fort-Brescia, and Laurinda Spear, these last serving as the designers of the house.

The house is poised on the edge of the Biscayne Bay in a suburb made up of ranch houses interspersed with occasional larger residences executed in a debased art deco manner. The garden is enclosed on all sides by a white rendered blockwork wall. The formality of the short gravel drive leading up to the house is reinforced by a line of six royal palms stretching across the facade to form a natural colonnade. These trees and the stepped formation of the blockwork at the gateway set a tone that is at once formal, playful, and yet at the same time, discreet.

Despite the axial approach, the building is asymmetrical, the entrance being through an elevated portico set to one side of the central axis. A stair with a stepped balustrade provides access to the raised entry level, and one enters the house through a narrow forecourt containing a pool that is shielded from the sun by a suspended canvas awning. The presence of the pool is indicated on the main facade by a circular porthole beneath the water, and by a glass-block wall illuminated by the changing play of reflected light coming off the water.

227

This partly permeable frontal facade, painted dark red, ochre, and pink with white window frames, is only the first in a series of screenlike layers. The next layer accommodates the lap pool and a separate master bedroom with its own balcony facing the front garden together with a study-suite adjacent to the entrance. This courtyard is flanked by an access corridor feeding the main rooms of the house.

Equipped with full-height doors opening onto a pool court, this double-height corridor serves as another layer that terminates at its extremities in straight flights of stairs that give access to the narrow first floor above. One of these stairs leads up to a gallery serving three bedrooms, a bathroom, and a walk-in closet. The other stair leads to an independent bedroom/bathroom with a balcony opening onto the bay.

228

All of the bedrooms, except the one adjacent to the entry court, give onto the water, as do the main rooms of the house on the elevated ground floor comprising the sitting room, music room, dining room, kitchen, breakfast terrace, and maid's quarters.

These spatial layers, in conjunction with the open-air courtyard and pool, turn the entire house into a light modulator that responds to every aspect of natural light.

The interior is painted a very pale blue-gray, which makes the internal layers and surfaces particularly susceptible to changes in the angle and the intensity of the light. From one instant to the next these planes radiate with sunlight while the intervening glazed membranes cast sharply etched shadows or are suffused with a soft rose tint that turns to a cold, watery gray as low-angle rays penetrate the portico and courtyard from the southwest. All of this is enriched by broken, faceted light coming off the pool when it is in use.

The composition of the house is remarkable for the way in which its all but neoclassical symmetry is asymmetrically inflected. This is particularly evident on approaching the house from the water. From here the underlying symmetrical structure is evident, with stairs leading down a paved terrace, left and right. This double-height elevation breaks down into a centered row of four large squares, the first of which frames the breakfast terrace while the last encloses the music room, comprising a double-height curtain wall broken into a grid of squares by glazing bars. Between these two full-height squares—the one open and the other closed—lie two other squares, divided into four squares each, which effectively frame the kitchen and dining room and bedrooms above, while a central recessed balcony running the full width of the bedrooms opens out to the bay. While the rest of the house is painted red ochre, this waterfront facade is painted white.

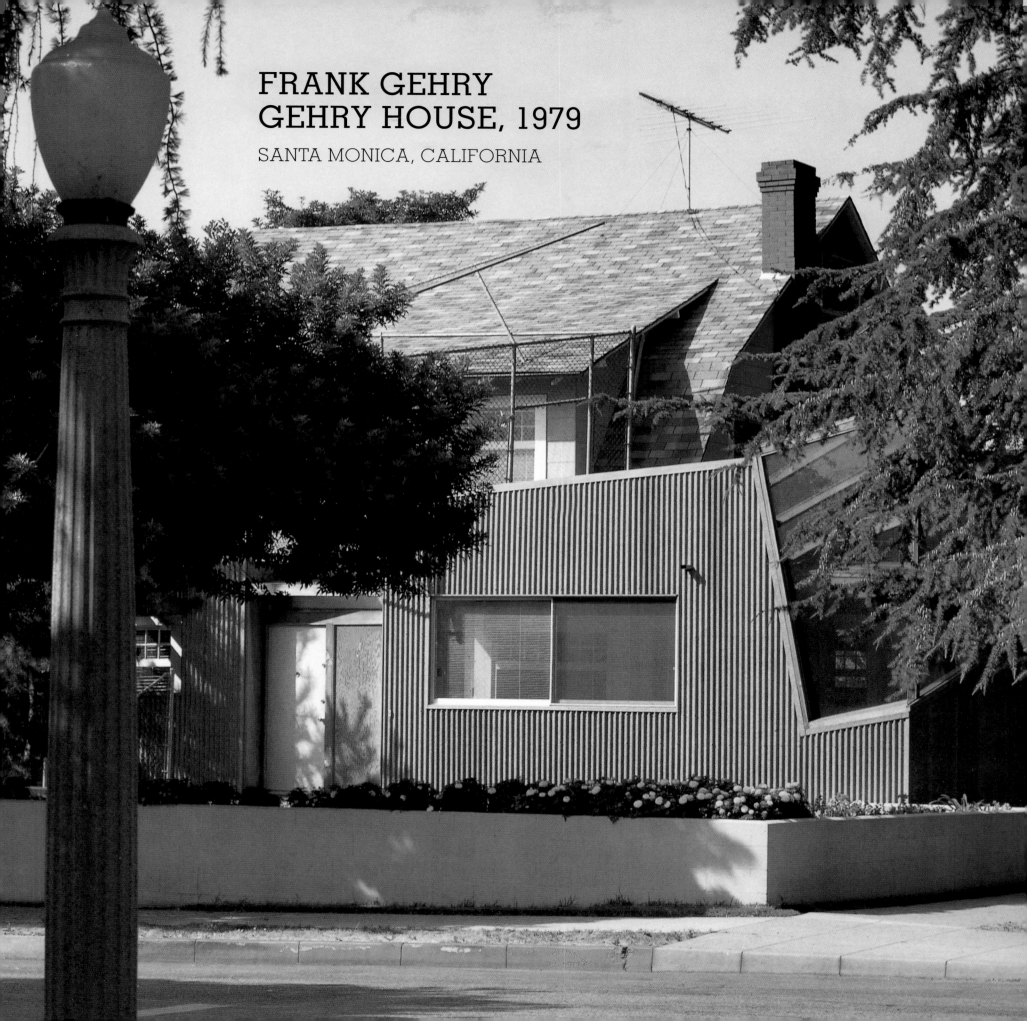

FRANK GEHRY
GEHRY HOUSE, 1979

SANTA MONICA, CALIFORNIA

Designed for the architect's own occupation in the late 1970s, this residence is an ironic recontextualization of an ordinary suburban house dating from the early twentieth century. Inspired by Venturi's populist cult of the "dumb and the ordinary," which Gehry had first employed in his Santa Monica Place shopping center of 1975, the architect elected to expose the anatomy of the balloon frame and then cover its partially disemboweled form in a new, loose collaged enclosure made up of the materials of the American strip—a corrugated iron sheet and chain-link fencing. By resorting to these materials Gehry simultaneously challenged the fictitious middle-class status of the typical suburban house and threw into question the entire problematic condition of the American megalopolis.

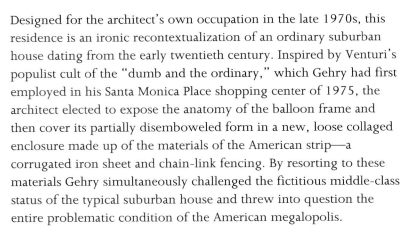

Using the literally "deconstructive strategy" pioneered by the artist Gordon Matta-Clark, Gehry created an extremely ambiguous image. It was always hard to tell on approaching it whether one was in the presence of an abandoned ruin or a building under construction.

The Gehry house is a particularly refined, lyrical collage of found elements with many antecedents in the rich history of twentieth-century art and architecture. The delicate, planar interweaving of corrugated iron, chain link, wired glass, exposed stud frame, and old siding evokes the work of Kurt Schwitters—not only his famous Merzbau but also his elegant collages made out of the detritus of the industrial city. It is but a step from Schwitters at one moment in the century to Robert Rauschenberg in another, a step that Gehry attempted to translate into contemporary architectural culture with this collage of exposed stud framing, red-cedar rafters, and roofing felt. Certain sectors of this ruin were left provocatively inaccessible such as the network of exposed rafters under the eaves. On the other hand, since the original house was enlarged by the extensive additions, certain conventional features normally associated with the exterior find themselves marooned within, such as a former external window that now, reglazed with mirror glass, finds itself reincarnated as a medicine cabinet.

Gehry shifted the symbolic core of the house from the former living room, which remained where it was, to the top-lit kitchen addition suspended between an outer shell of corrugated iron and the original balloon frame. This space was capped by a wood-framed glass cube that from a distance appeared fallen out of the main body of the original house, thereby providing both a skylight and a bay window for the new kitchen-dining volume.

Gehry's approach depends upon the total dissolution of the boundaries separating architecture from art. His peculiarly sculptural sensibility has influenced a number of younger architects in Southern California, among them Frank Israel, and he has become, however inadvertently, the founder of a new California school that, through his daring example, happened upon a willful, irreverent, and seemingly popular alternative to the high modernism of the twentieth-century avant-garde.

236

KRUECK & OLSON
STEEL & GLASS HOUSE, 1980
CHICAGO, ILLINOIS

Emerging out of the Miesian courtyard-house tradition, this lavish dwelling was designed, according to the client's brief, to provide suburban conditions in the middle of the city. To this end, the mass of the house is articulated about three courts: a forecourt distancing the principal facade from the street, a central patio, and a garden court set to the rear of the sixty-seven-by-one-hundred-twenty-seven-foot plot.

As much influenced by the Californian Case Study houses as by Mies van der Rohe, with a sideways glance at Pierre Chareau's Maison de Verre, this house is made up of a series of translucent layers and by a rather labyrinthine approach to circulation, both of which serve to remove it from the Miesian IIT tradition to which Krueck so evidently belongs.

240

The house clearly owes much to the utilitarian works that Mies designed for the IIT campus, above all, perhaps, the boiler house and the Minerals and Metals Building, both dating from 1943.

While the rigor of the exposed structural frame patently stems from Mies, the metal grill screening of the double-height entrance combined with the sinuous mode of entry establishes the subtle contrapuntal tone of the house as it unfolds in depth. Thus on entering, one passes first to the right and then to the left, first encountering the stair leading to the second floor past a glimpse of the patio terrace that deftly extends the space of the foyer. After these initial shifts, the main circulatory route realigns with the main east-west axis to enter the living room. This seventy-foot-long double-height space extends almost without interruption into the single-story dining area and conservatory, affording access simultaneously to the breakfast room, kitchen, and servants' wing.

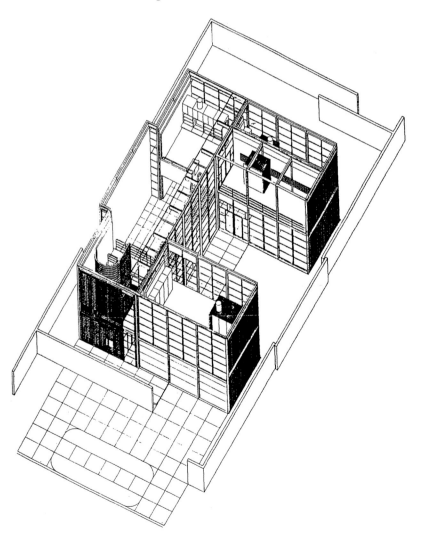

The second-floor itinerary is as serpentine as that of the first, at least until one reaches the glass-lensed, steel-framed passerelle bridging over the living room beside the central patio. A frosted glass skylight above, of the same width and set exactly above this bridge, provides natural light to the floor below. Since this is adjacent to the south-facing curtain wall of the patio, the surplus light has to be modulated by roller blinds. Different transparencies permeate the house, combined with tectonic articulations that serve to heighten a series of incidental but integrated set pieces. Among these are the glazed drum of the main stair as it forms one end of the living volume and the cacti conservatory that surely alludes to Mies's Tugendhat House of 1930. As Nory Miller has remarked, these episodes, together with their furnishings, are constantly transformed by the changing play of light:

Light is one thing by day, another at night. Just as the solids and voids reverse themselves . . . so does the palette undergo transformation. By day, the colors are very cool . . . vague in-between colors: pink-beiges, blue-greens and grays that turn blue one hour, violet the next. At night, the interior turns golden.

244

Subtly landscaped in the minimalist spirit of the IIT master gardener Arthur Caldwell and exquisitely furnished with Miesian furniture and Donald Judd–like pieces designed by the architects, this house, precisely executed in rich materials, has been all too modestly described by Krueck as a realized "student thesis." It is, on the contrary, both an outstanding first work and a Miesian *repetition différence* of indisputable quality.

CARLOS JIMÉNEZ
ARCHITECT'S HOUSE AND STUDIO, 1983–2007, HOUSTON, TEXAS

This unique instance of suburban infill development began with an extremely modest single-story, pitched-roof dwelling of around five hundred square feet in area. This starter unit was gradually transformed not only into a two-story dwelling six times its original size but also into two separate dwellings facing each other, respectively designated and used as the primary residence and the architect's studio. This elaborate transformation was achieved in seven phases over a twenty-four-year period, the penultimate phase being the moment in 1993 when Carlos Jiménez bought a second suburban lot of similar dimensions opposite the original site. The architect built his present house on this second lot, beginning with a two-story unit running parallel to the street frontage, which is now augmented by a single-story unit extending at right angles into the garden. In this house, realized in two stages, the original two-story unit facing the street accommodates a kitchen/dining/living space above with bedrooms below. The final addition of a generous kitchen/dining/

living volume to the rear, facing out over a garden terrace, enables the ground floor of the original unit to remain as bedrooms, with a new main bedroom-cum-study suite above.

With the completion of this addition, Jiménez will purchase another lot adjacent to the site of the original house, thereby providing the architect's studio with an ample garden. Although the current state of the complex is now divided between a studio on one side of Willard Street and a house on the other, it is clear that both units could equally serve as private residences, so that the current division of usage could be reversed, if it were necessary, in the future.

No one has written more appreciatively of these serial transformations than the Houston architecture critic Darrell Fields, particularly with regard to the initial house and its incremental modification during the years 1983 to 1986:

For Jiménez, Houston is not as relentless as it would appear to the rest of us. It exists in very discrete places, and these places are imbued by their author with other phenomenal attributes. . . . The Houston that Jiménez constructs is not a false reading, it is a private one. . . . The most essential frame is the frame of privacy represented by the studio itself. For example, in reflecting on the first iteration (1983), it is unclear as to whether we are looking at the plan of a small residence or a studio. Perhaps it is a studio-home or apartment in the most literal and functional sense. It is not until we compare the first iteration with the second (1984), however, that we discover that the "studio" component, through some programmatic necessity, has been doubled and displaced to the upper left of the site plan. This dislocation produces three primary effects. First, it reveals the fact that there was a private realm (studio) superimposed on a domestic one (house). Second, it produces, between the first component and the second, a more articulated space separating the aforementioned architectonic events. Third, it clarifies the typological condition of the "studio" as a single room for an individual. . . .

249

Fields is alluding at this juncture to the 1984 erection of a single studio in the garden of the first lot, to be followed in 1986 with the building of an architectural office as a third freestanding studio on the same site. At this point, what had been the studio in 1984 became the library while the office went on to serve as the studio. Fields notes that while all three units are barely more than a few feet apart, the architect still had to walk to work, so to speak. For Fields, as for the architect, these detached freestanding units simulate a micro-urban space between them, although this tended to disappear once the studio was linked to the library in 1991. A further expansion of the

original studio/house in 1997 finally yielded a continuous mass form and inner route around an existing pecan tree, which Jiménez was to maintain through all the multifarious modifications that took place over a decade and a half. Between 1999 and 2007, Jiménez modified the internal arrangement while simultaneously slightly reducing the overall footprint.

In all these various comings and goings a discrete modern language has been sustained throughout, passing imperceptibly between the somewhat metaphysical aedicule of his first miniature house and

studio, inspired by the Italian architect Aldo Rossi and the bold severity of the current minimalist syntax. No one has captured the layered significance of all these changes better than the architect himself when he wrote in 2003:

We inhabit a world whose perceptions are often manipulated by the distorting mirror of speed and instant gratification. Yet what is most compelling about architecture is that, despite the dominance of such cultural propensities, its innumerable pleasures unfold slowly. Constructed over gradual, sometimes ineffable, accumulations of time, architecture becomes a vital framework for dwelling in the world; and dwelling ultimately reveals architecture's irrepressible humanity. In an age filled with countless marvels, architecture continues to astonish primarily because the alchemy of its

fundamental materials—light, space, and time—enrich, as few other things can, the very experience of life. . . .

My house and studio are a living thing. Their simple, container-like forms hold a thousand memories and a thousand more to be. Every day I look forward to crossing the street between each building, encountering on either short journey something I have never seen before, something I have seen countless times. As I write these lines, Houston's early spring saturates the city with the supplest tonalities of green. I am reminded of other springs, of other architectures, of the forgiving aroma of the sea. The world always moves slowly across the enormous weight of each day. Architecture invites moments of profound lightness; its volumes, its spaces, have the ability to ground us while revealing the ethereality of that which remains constant.

DAVID ROCKWOOD
ROCKWOOD HOUSE, 1984–1986, PORTLAND, OREGON

Of the many successors to the principal of off-the-peg prefabricated assembly as demonstrated in 1949 by Charles and Ray Eames in their Case Study House and Studio, few can compare to the modular resolution of this house designed by David Rockwood for his parents. The whole house has been formulated as a modular, partially prefabricated system that could in principle be applied to other buildings and building types. On the one hand, it is a neoplatonic minimalist work, wherein an orthogonal grid determines each coordinate. On the other, it is a technological tour de force in which each junction is resolved to provide an all but seamless network of joints.

Based on a vertical and horizontal grid of eleven feet six inches, the structural system comprises two interconnected concepts. In the first instance it consists of a three-dimensional structural grid made of six-by-six-inch hollow square sections in welded tubular steel; in the second, this matrix is filled-in with precast concrete sandwich panels that make up the floor, roof, and walls. The nine-and-a-half-inch-thick wall panels are ingeniously constructed out of two layers separated by three and a half inches of rigid polyurethane. This insulation is sandwiched between a three-and-a-half-inch load-bearing concrete wall on the interior and a three-inch layer of pumice concrete on the exterior, the whole being bound together by wire. The ten-inch-thick floor and roof panels are similarly constructed, beginning with a prefabricated two-and-a-half-inch reinforced-concrete panel topped by five inches of rigid insulation. Over this is then poured a two-and-a-half-inch field in-situ concrete roof.

Spatially and formally this house has many antecedents, ranging from Guiseppe Terragni's Casa del Fascio, which Rockwood acknowledges as a canonical model, to more formalist approaches as we find these in figures as diverse as Peter Eisenman and the Swiss architect Fritz Haller. One also senses the influence of the Maison de Verre in Paris, particularly in the use of glass-block panels for the side walls and the nine-square roof lights illuminating the double-height, internal atrium.

Entered from the east and to one side of a nine-square bay, this house unfolds on two floors to the north and south. To the north, on the ground floor, is the weaving studio and, above, an elevated living/dining/kitchen space overlooking the marina. Behind the atrium to the south is a garage and, above, the master bedroom with its private terrace. The decision to elevate the living floor derived from the conflict between the desirable view and the southern orientation, combined with the need to ensure privacy within a densely planned development. Fed by a single, straight flight of stairs, the main spaces are augmented on both floors by a service zone against the western wall comprising a darkroom and a guest suite on the ground floor and a kitchen and bathroom above.

Among the most refreshing aspects about this house are the points at which the architect departed from his system. This is most evident in the way in which the glass-block roof light is raised clear of the basic structure. Similar extra-structural articulations occur in the curtain walling on the eastern and northern elevations, where the plate-glass skin is set in front of the frame.

On the north facade, on the other hand, the glass fenestration is inserted into the frame. This inflection is further liberated on the northeast corner of the house, where a glass balustrade cantilevers beyond the frame to align with a freestanding chimney and an access ladder to the roof.

STANLEY SAITOWITZ
DE NAPOLI HOUSE
1987–1990

LOS GATOS, CALIFORNIA

Situated in the hills above Los Gatos and built on a wooded
promontory pointing north toward San Jose, the single story
De Napoli House is made of three parallel strands: a swimming pool
and master wing; a living room and garden court; and a dining/
kitchen volume plus secondary bedrooms and services. These layers
slide past one another as they align themselves along the ribbed
contours of the site. Inspired by Machu Picchu and also by Mies van
der Rohe and by the Mexican architect Luis Barragán, the De Napoli
residence is more of an earthwork than a house in the traditional
sense. Everything here depends on the play of various terraces and
rooms at slightly different levels, a syncopation entailing subtle but
telling changes in datum throughout. The result is a stepped podium
in fair-faced stone that in its topographic character resembles the
articulation of landscape that Mies first projected in his Brick Country
House project of 1924. Out of such influences Saitowitz has created
a new work, the freshness and grandeur of which has rarely been
equaled in recent years.

This house is distinguished by the calm with which the various rooms are assembled in a linear manner in relation to both earthwork and waterwork, with different parts of the residence being hierarchically differentiated through different modes of construction. Thus, the main living pavilion in the center of the complex is of steel-framed construction with large plate-glass windows, an oversailing roof, and sheet-metal fascias. The secondary side wings, on the other hand, are of more traditional wood-framed stucco construction.

Since the roofscape of the house forms a fifth elevation, particularly as this may be observed from the upper "barn/guest house," which is also the main point of entry into the site, the treatment of the roof terraces had to be given careful consideration. It was decided that whether paved or covered in gravel, they should not be penetrated by vents and drains. To this end the architect, with the aid of the contractor, developed an ingenious system of covered channels and concealed outlets passing through the parapets of adjacent walls. The fall also had to be minimized in order to reduce the thickness of the fascias as much as possible.

The narrow end of the promontory is defined by a small pool house and belvedere, both of which serve to terminate the horizontal thrust of the house as it points toward the horizon.

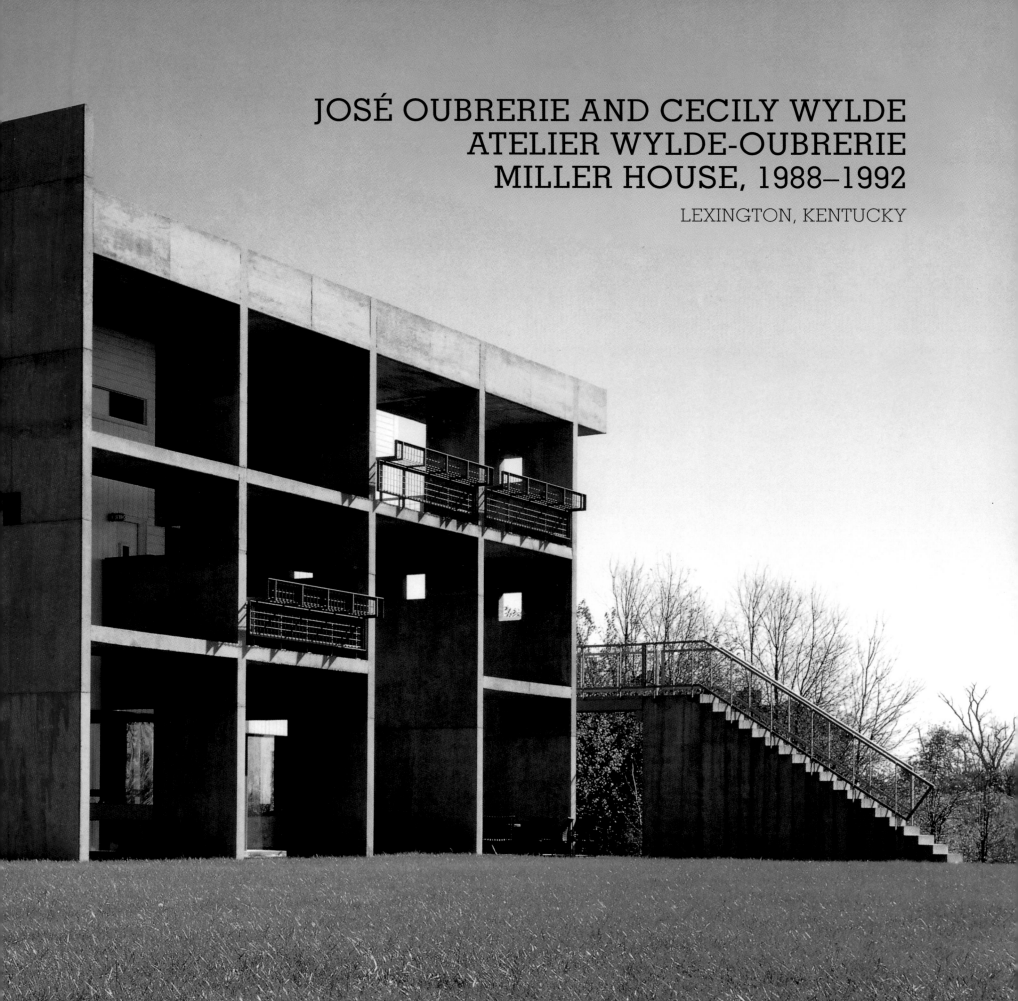

JOSÉ OUBRERIE AND CECILY WYLDE
ATELIER WYLDE-OUBRERIE
MILLER HOUSE, 1988–1992

LEXINGTON, KENTUCKY

Designed by a former assistant of Le Corbusier, this is a work of exceptional complexity and plastic richness. It is essentially a pinwheeling, fugal composition in space that also happens to be a luxurious house designed to accommodate a family: a lawyer, his wife, and their two children. All four at various times live and work in different parts of the country so this house is intended as their home base. It comprises three small double-height, cubic houses suspended within the free-flowing space of a single orthogonal envelope, while the ground floor and the roof establish the upper and lower datums of the overall prism. All four elevations are subject to planar displacements, and the southeast and northwest faces in particular feature first-floor catwalks and stairways that jut out into the landscape.

These dynamic elements reinforce the spiraling character of the house so that as one moves around, the components of each elevation group themselves into a different compositional relationship. A three-quarter view of the house from the north imparts a feeling of modesty and compactness, interrupted only by the cantilevered entrance canopy and concrete elevator shaft. When viewed from the south across the pond, the house breaks down into its two opposing forms: the main concrete mass that incorporates the *brise-soleil*, facing southwest, and a white clapboarded timber box that seems to rotate within the concrete frame and occasionally rise to its face. One may see in this interplay a conscious opposition between European *béton brut* construction and the American balloon frame.

274

As seen from the south and southwest, the concrete sunshades inevitably recall Le Corbusier's Mill Owners Building built in Ahmedabad in 1956. These *brise-soleil* impart a peculiarly monumental character to the house that seems to be borne out by the interior treatment. Thus it is hardly a surprise to discover on entering the house that the main floor has been rendered as a surrogate public realm. The three separate, double-height bedroom suites, each suspended above the living room on cylindrical columns, connect with the main floor via a continuous first-floor walkway that starts with a dog-leg stair in the western corner of the house and extends to a catwalk stair leading out into the greensward. Each bedroom suite has its own bathroom while the bedrooms themselves are capped by an auxiliary living loft above the lower sleeping level.

shell and its peripheral surfaces as a subset of the main house. The cabinetwork also evokes the Maison de Verre in that closets, cabinets, and fittings of every kind were progressively detailed as the construction proceeded. The peculiarly rich, tailor-made effect obviously stems from the unusual working method and provides, as in the work of Carlo Scarpa, a level of articulation that could not be achieved in any other way. Air-conditioning tubes and ducts that dramatically interpenetrate the volume render the house as a kind of elaborate servo-mechanism. This utilitarian atmosphere is heightened by the square-gridded, wire-mesh balustrading used throughout. The architects balance this machinism with high-quality woodwork in birch and beech and colored wall planes (predominantly red, blue, and green) that cause the space to dilate.

Looking up at the first-floor circulation or into the innumerable slots that separate the bedroom suites from one another and also from the intersticial circulation, one is irresistibly reminded of Pierre Chareau's Maison de Verre, not only because of the vertical character of the interpenetrating space but also because of the collagelike approach applied throughout, with every component being literally laid into the

This contrapuntal perceptual play is enlivened throughout by horizontal slots, square picture windows, and plate-glass corner fenestration. Each of these window types provides a distinctive frame for the views over the surrounding countryside.

276

Two other elements assure a sense of intimacy and homeliness in a house that is otherwise almost institutional in scale and feeling. The first of these is a central fireplace that, backing onto the entry foyer, serves to establish a hearth for the entire family.

The second feature is the private terrace of the master bedroom, facing
south/southeast, that affords a particularly intimate view over the
lake. From this terrace one may descend via a timber catwalk and stair
to the lawn surrounding the house and from there to the lake itself.

SMITH-MILLER AND HAWKINSON
HOUSE FOR A FILM PRODUCER,
1989–1991

LOS ANGELES, CALIFORNIA

It is hard to imagine a more appropriate occasion for a partial return to the values of the California Case Study houses than the revamping of this Neutra-like house, dating from the early 1960s, particularly since the original house was designed by Donald Polsky, who had been apprenticed to Neutra.

Smith-Miller and Hawkinson gave this three-bedroom, single-story house, situated on a spectacular site, a totally different proportion by stripping the house back to its basic frame and by superimposing a new master bedroom and deck on top of the original skeleton. In addition to this crowning superstructure, the architects extended the

house laterally with terraces and gardens, including a garden of perennials on the street front, executed by the landscape-designer–architect Akva Stein. The entry to the house is bounded by sandblasted stone walls of varying height and further articulated by two timber pergolas set at different heights, one of them serving as a canopy for the main approach. Adjacent to this is a two-car garage.

The orthogonal order of the front of the house gives way on the interior to a series of interconnected living spaces of rather loose configuration.

Each space flows into the next, although they can be broken down into separate volumes by use of sliding and sliding-folding walls. These isolate certain sectors such as the media room and kitchen. Retractable, spring-loaded canvas sunshades and sliding-glass doors modify the perimeter of the house and increase the sense of a seemingly boundless exterior. This free space finally terminates in a series of decks and a swimming pool set at some distance from the house.

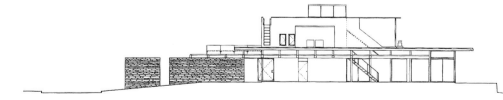

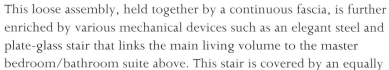

This loose assembly, held together by a continuous fascia, is further enriched by various mechanical devices such as an elegant steel and plate-glass stair that links the main living volume to the master bedroom/bathroom suite above. This stair is covered by an equally crystalline glass roof. A monopitched operable skylight is situated to the side of the stair while a rail extends the implied volume onto the bedroom deck.

Both bedroom and deck are furnished with classic Eames furniture and treated as an elevated living space. A split in the ceiling height of the living volume makes one aware of the bedroom level above. Gray wood, aluminum trim, and custom carpeting unify these various elisions, along with the use of such materials as stainless steel for the fireplace surround and sandblasted lexan for the garage doors. The aura of machinism is reinforced by such diminutive devices as a sliding shaving mirror that enables the user to look at himself and the panorama simultaneously.

Like Neutra's Kaufmann House in Palm Springs, this house literally dissolves into the surrounding landscape. However, unlike Neutra's work, it also seems to float above the ground like a spaceship. Despite this somewhat dramatic posture, the house emanates an attitude that is close in spirit to such minimalists as Donald Judd and Dan Flavin. This laconic, almost diffident matter-of-factness sets the house apart from the straitlaced, productive functionalism of the earlier Southern California School.

MARK MACK
SUMMERS HOUSE,
1990

SANTA MONICA, CALIFORNIA

Modeled after an adobe village, this residential complex comprises a house and studio separated by a forecourt with a swimming pool. One enters this courtyard from the south under a timber pergola at the end of the studio building. The latter houses a guest room, a music room, and a library, while serving symbolically as a gatehouse. The main house beyond, raised on a shallow podium, breaks up into a series of elevated decks and attendant rooms. The first tier in this stacked assembly comprises a barbecue patio overlooking the pool. This patio is flanked by the living, dining, and family rooms of the house. Access to a second terrace, raised a full floor above the first, is via an open wooden staircase, a feature that is echoed by an almost identical flight leading to a practice room at the top of the house.

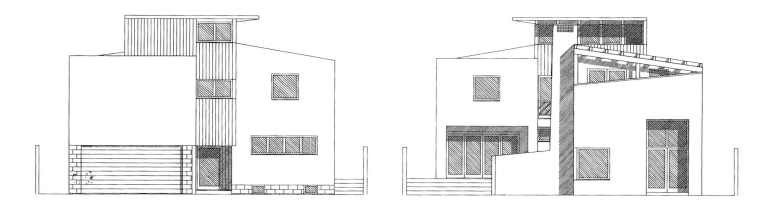

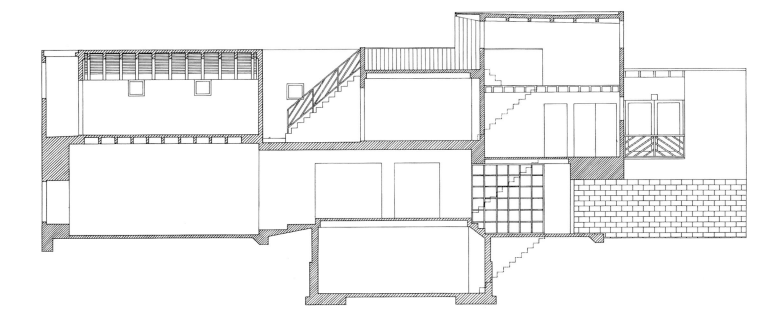

Designed for a family of musicians, the Summers house was conceived after the Loosian space-planning principle in which the levels of adjacent rooms are invariably displaced slightly in relation to each other, creating a sensation of increasing or decreasing volume as one passes from one space to the next. This spatial hierarchy helps to produce the required sense of informality or formality in the various rooms. Thus, above the low entry from the north, two floors of low-ceilinged rooms are accommodated within a twenty-eight-foot-high zoning envelope, while on the south the house rises for two somewhat higher floors. These honorific south-facing rooms comprise a main living space at grade and a high-ceilinged master bedroom above. The arrangement of the rooms on the second floor follows that of a typical patio house, with the four-bed-three-bath sequence grouped around a central patio and a practice room. An internal stair leads from this level to a second practice room at the top of the house.

The exterior, rendered in red and yellow ochre, gray-blue, and pink, and offset by timberwork stained acid green, has a radiant appearance reminiscent of the work of the Mexican architect Luis Barragán, who has exercised a profound influence on Mack. However, this polychromatic treatment is carried into the interior in a manner that departs from Barragán and bears a resemblance to the chromatic spatial effects of the Dutch De Stijl movement.

The architect's attitude is more playful, however, and by abandoning
the exclusive use of primary colors favored by the Dutch, Mack was able
to indulge in an irridescent mixture of yellows and greens, particularly
in the kitchen and bathroom, combined with red panels and blue
mosaics around the bath itself. The effect is of a magically illuminated
coziness possessed of a self-conscious, folkloric dimension that
unexpectedly recalls the work of the Austrian painter Hundertwasser.

Raised and educated in Austria, Mack shifted his ground, moving from the concrete-block, quasi-Palladian, neoprimitivism of his early San Francisco practice with Andrew Batey to the fuller, more open, collagist palette of his Southern California work. His buildings became relaxed assemblies of somewhat random components: chevroned pergola spans, diagonal balustrading, exposed timber rafters, cross-braced panels, plywood and timber siding, plaster walls, and flat and inclined roofs in metal with standing seams.

ANTOINE PREDOCK
FULLER HOUSE,
1986–1987

PHOENIX, ARIZONA

Not since Frank Lloyd Wright first ventured into Scottsdale in 1932 to set up his winter headquarters in Taliesin West has any architect evoked with comparable intensity the myth of America's aboriginal past and of the desert in which it is inscribed. Predock's approach is quintessentially topographic, as the following passage makes abundantly clear:

In the Southwest, I always think of the fundamental connection between earth and sky, through the mute blank adobe walls that you find here. This has influenced me enormously. There is such a completeness in adobe architecture; the wall acts as a bridge between earth and sky. It is of the earth, an extension of the earth aspiring toward the sky, and any sort of decorative addition, a cornice or a stringcourse, would feel secondary and half-hearted compared to the power of the wall itself. . . . Sometimes a building's connection to place starts with a silhouette. When we come to the West for the first time and try to get our bearings, there is a daunting confrontation—the limitless landscape, a limitless sky, distant mountain ranges iconically marking the land. I understand the tendency towards monumentality, ersatz monumentality, when confronted by the onslaught of this infinite space. How does one go up against a mountain range? One option is to make something comfortable like a classical pediment, the impulse that had traditionally been followed in false-front western towns. Another option, one that I have chosen, is to make buildings that suggest an analogous landscape.

Like a great deal of Wright's work, the two-bedroom, three-car Fuller House appears to be much larger than it actually is. Spread-eagled over the floor of the desert, it erupts in unexpected ways against the ubiquitous backdrop of cacti and straggly shrubs. Certain salient features, among them the central pyramid and two belvedere viewing towers at either end of the house, help to create the impression of a vast, rambling complex set amid boulders and scrub. According to Predock these features correspond to the cosmic, astrological setting of the house in the following ways:

This project links east and west with a sunrise terrace and a sunset tower. A source of water is contained in the space between. Daily living patterns shift from morning to evening: morning areas are to the east, and evening spaces, with vantage points for viewing the sunset, to the west. Boulders tumble into the courtyard, suggesting a dance, or the poetic tension between landscape and architecture: whether the landscape will subsume the building, as at Angkor Wat or Chaco Canyon. That tension is frozen here. Inside, water issues from a black granite monolith and runs through a channel parallel to the east-west axis of the house. The water's path culminates in a quiet pool in the courtyard. The pool recalls a lake in a valley of boulders. A "crossfire" of water marks the entry, connecting visually with the black channel inside. The house is axially

positioned in relation to the east-west travel of the sun. Winter sun penetration is maximized and low summer sun angles are excluded. Trellises filter light across the sandstone floors. The house is set deeply into the earth to provide thermal stability. Its views skim across the surface of the desert. The higher vantage points, like the sunset tower, have views across the valley toward the nighttime lights of Phoenix, to the sunset in the west and to the mountains in the east.

Rather than being hierarchized in either a classical or a modernist sense, the Fuller House is decentralized and multicentered, with various rooms of sometimes odd and unexpected shapes leading disjointedly from one episode to the next. The zoning of the house is also rather unusual: one enters from the north between a three-car garage and a monumental stair to confront a black stone monolith, set on the cross axis of a long hallway, with a watercourse running east-west toward a circular pool and garden terrace that is the nexus of the scheme. There is at this point in the plan a hidden opposition between the monumentality of the water axis, slowly descending toward the pool, and the intimate familial acommodations stacked on either side of the route, that is, the kitchen, breakfast and dining rooms and other ancillary spaces that back on to the garage. These intimate provisions aside, the house consists of three monumental spaces directly served by the long hall. Respectively, from south to north, these are a study, excised out of the pyramid that stands adjacent to the pool, a media room raised slightly above the hall, and a radially shaped living room that looks through the bounding loggia to the courtyard beyond. Thereafter the house breaks up into spaces of greater intimacy, comprising the master bedroom/bathroom complex and a guest room located at the western end of the house.

The most dramatic and most symbolic aspect of the house is the central pyramid, which, as Henry Plummer has observed, is unmistakably masonic, an ironic allusion even to the Great Seal of the United States. At once all-seeing eye and pyramidon, the top of this pyramid forms the pyramidal skylight to the study beneath. According to Egyptian legend, this is the point at which the Phoenix alights at dawn at the beginning of each day. Irrespective of such associations, this aperture clearly functions as an inverted sundial, since the sunlight that enters the study also effectively registers the time of day until it drops so low as to disappear from view.

Faced in the purple-pinkish adoquin stone of the nearby mountain, the surface of the pyramid divides into three separate layers: first into the thirteen tiered steps that cover the base like an inverted amphitheater; second, into a smooth face executed in the same stone as the base; and finally, into the glazed pyramidon.

Set well into the ground to capitalize on its thermal mass and built out of thick layers of concrete and concrete block to shield the interior from the intense heat and cold of the desert, this house is inspired as much by the Middle East as by any evocation of local lore—hence the twin-stelae standing just outside the house at the eastern end of the transverse axis and the water channels running east-west and south-north to terminate in the circular reflecting pool. According to the architect, the first of these is meant to represent culture, while the second is supposed to evoke the sovereignty of nature. A similar dualism appears in the sunrise and sunset loggias raised on the roof at either end of the east-west axis, the one semi-public and the other linked to the privacy of the bedroom wing. Rendered gray ochre on the exterior and cream within, the house, screened throughout by latticework fenestration, is a constantly changing field of light.

309

RICARDO
LEGORRETA

GREENBERG
HOUSE,
1991

LOS ANGELES,
CALIFORNIA

This is one of a number of Southern California houses that Ricardo Legoretta has designed since the mid-1980s. Legoretta's point of departure amounts to a total repudiation in the received aesthetic of the modern Californian house as this has evolved over the past seventy years at the hands of Richard Neutra, Rudolph Schindler, J. R. Davidson, Charles Eames, and Craig Ellwood. As with Legoretta's Montalban House, Hollywood, of 1985, and the so-called Casa de Rancho of 1987, the Greenberg House consists of massive, mostly blank walls enclosing inner volumes and various atria and rendered, inside and out, in virtually the same tone and texture of ochre-colored plaster. Legoretta sharpens this earth-toned palette here and there with reentrant walls tinted in magenta, lavender, and cerise. With a wall-to-window-area ratio of at least twenty to one, Legoretta has made here the first concerted effort since Wright's textile-block houses to remind Californians that they do in fact live in a desert.

As with its predecessors of the late 1980s, the Greenberg House strikes a dynamic balance between an introspective atrium house that faces toward its own deftly concealed courtyards and an outriding terraced earthwork on which the house sits, replete with water basins, pergolas, and belvedere-patios looking out over the surrounding views. The terraced earthwork and the enclosing walls fuse with each other, rising and falling like dramatic, shadowed masses in relation to the landscape. While Legoretta has inherited this Iberian-Arabic, modernist syntax from his Mexican master, Luis Barragán, he adds to this legacy a massive plasticity of unmatched boldness and generosity, combined with a flare for color and light that is surely his own. There is nothing petty or trivial about this architecture and Legoretta has brought to the late twentieth century a sense of luxurious simplicity and calm that is unmatched in our time.

Derived from Legorreta's earlier work in Mexico, above all his Camino Real Hotel in Mexico City of 1967, the poetics of this dwelling do not turn on the fine materials but rather on the play of texture, shadow, and light. These all but imperceptible phenomena create spaces that are tranquil as well as elegant.

312

The internal circulation is enriched by large picture windows and relatively small openings deftly and unexpectedly dispersed throughout. These windows, which may seem random at first, are strategically located: they either frame carefully isolated views of the landscape or bring a refreshing and unexpected shaft of light into the interior, depending on the time of day. The framed panorama beyond is equally subject to variations in the play and level of light, and the house subtly heightens these effects. This constantly varying luminosity is further enhanced by the use of simple materials and colors.

The floors are paved with Mexican tiles throughout, producing a slightly undulating and waxy surface in strong contrast to the dry, woven texture of the occasional rugs. These elements, together with the rough-textured plaster on the walls, guarantee a very mellow and absorbent acoustical tone.

In these atypical but luxurious modern dwellings Legoretta has introduced into the American mainstream a critical ethic derived from Barragán, who wrote more than forty years ago:

To a greater degree than Barragán and perhaps more than any other contemporary architect, Legoretta has transcended the all too confusing opposition between high art and popular culture, particularly as this applies to domestic architecture. This reconciliation stems from the quietly ludic character of Legoretta's architecture that in its turn derives from the fundamental economy of a traditional constructional method that is all too readily and foolishly dismissed as "primitive."

318

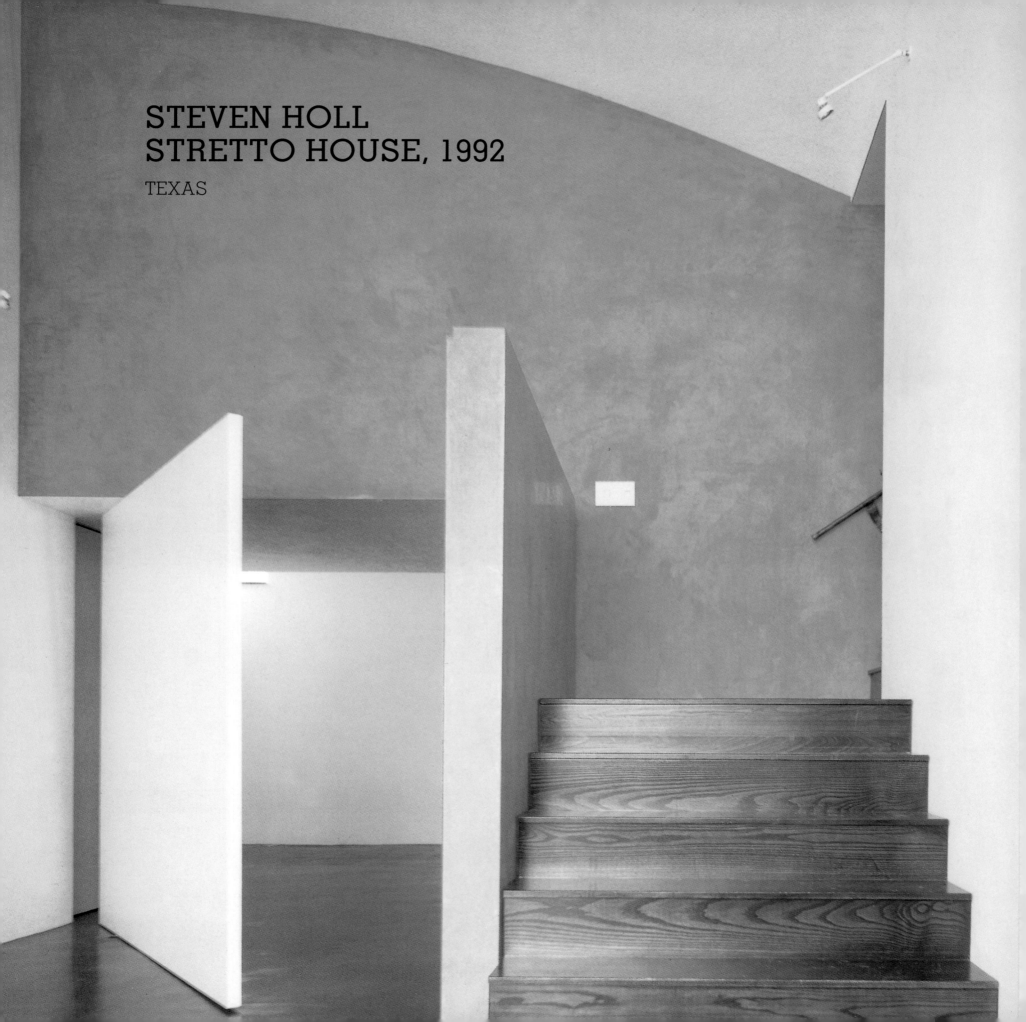

STEVEN HOLL
STRETTO HOUSE, 1992

TEXAS

In many respects the Stretto House derives quite directly from the characteristics of its unique site, a parcel of land partially flooded with three spring-fed ponds with dams that progressively feed the water through the grounds. Holl exploits these linked topographic elements as an elaborate metaphor for the spatial structuring of the house. Thus, the conceptual framework of this dwelling comprises "spatial dams" and "aqueous spaces" in which the "dams," made of concrete-block rectangular forms, are all too directly related to the concrete dams in the site. Between these orthogonal dams, metal framed "aqueous spaces," with curvilinear ceiling planes, are conceived as symbolizing the cyclical flow of the water through the pond. Together the longitudinal concrete boxes and the light roofs make for a lyrical composition that echoes the land-form.

One of the so-called "dams" is, in fact, an exterior room with a roof
terrace from which one can look over the ponds. A second external
room is not occupied, however, since it is filled with surplus pond
water. Holl refers to this space as the "flooded room," having in
mind scenes from Andre Tarkovsky's film *Stalker*. This space is
conceived and designed as the main point of intersection between
the house and the waterscape.

322

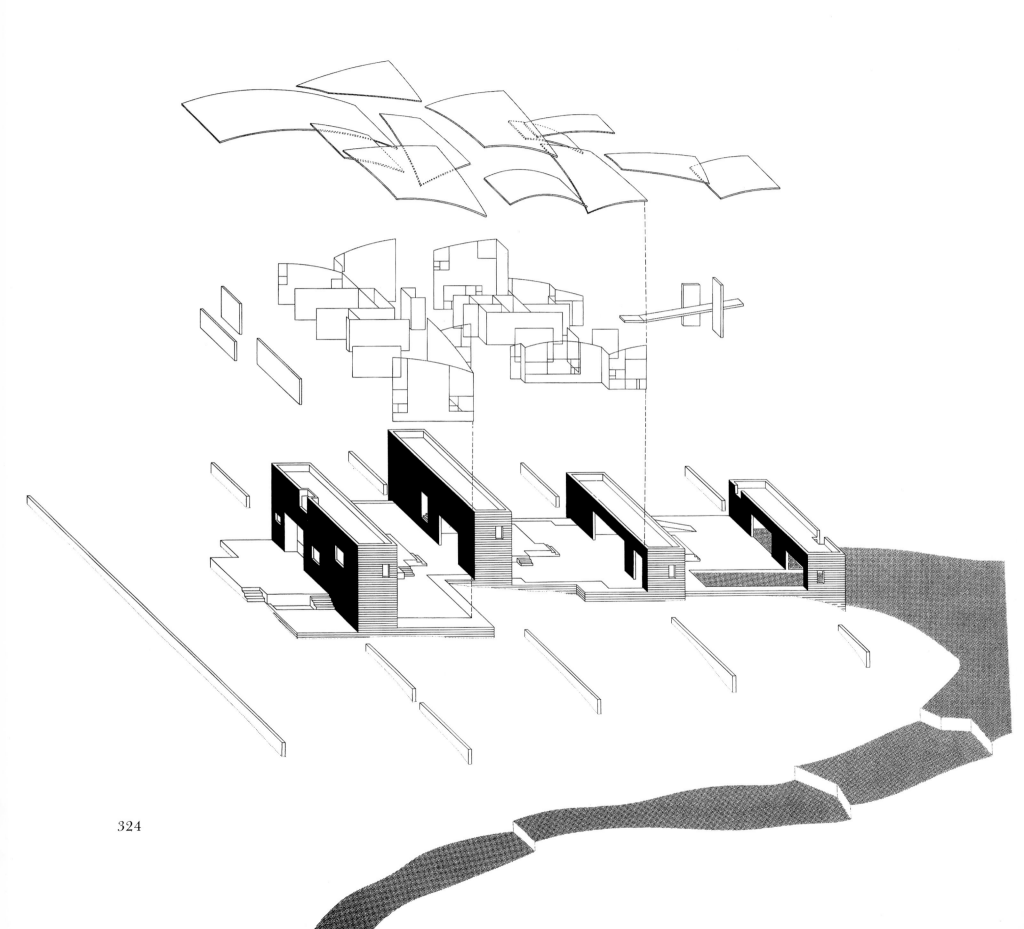

324

With the single exception of the master bedroom, dwelling takes place on the ground floor with subtle changes in level distinguishing one realm from the next. As one moves through these spaces one has a sense of moving through a series of garden pavilions.

As is typical of Holl's work in general, the interior of the house is not only inflected through level changes and differences in the intensity and direction of the light but also through the juxtaposition of different materials and colors. Both the entry and the internal surface of the house are enriched through the application of acid etched metal sheet and through the finishing of carefully selected planes in *stucco lucido*. The overall color scheme of these finishes passes from copper aluminum and opaque glass through to magenta-blue, whitened veridian, and a set of pale greens and yellows, all of which are constantly modified by the changing play of natural light that enters the house from different sides.

PETER BOHLIN, BERNARD CYWINSKI & JON JACKSON

LEDGE HOUSE, 1992–1996

CATOCTIN MOUNTAINS, MARYLAND

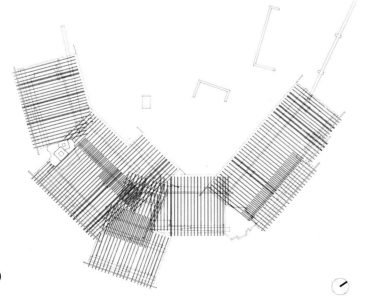

Along with an elaborate retreat realized in 1992 by the same architects near Lake George, New York, the Ledge House is a tour de force, which qualifies it as a masterwork in the old-fashioned sense of the term, rivaling the most extravagant private domains coming from the hands of leading American architects toward the end of the nineteenth century. I have in mind, in particular, Henry Hobson Richardson's Ames Gate Lodge, built in North Easton Massachusetts (1881). Like the Ames Gate Lodge, the Ledge House begins with an allusion to a more primordial past, the rooms unfolding in a broken sweep extending in two directions around a central forecourt and entry. In one direction, the sequence accommodates the master bedroom and study wing, while in the other it houses the children's bedrooms and an indoor swimming pool, situated to the northeast of the entrance.

Between these wings the visitor is confronted by a large living/
dining volume, plus a screened porch and kitchen set to one side.
The architects' description of the house and its siting merits citation
at length:

*Ledge House sits on a man-made ridge cut into the hillside that was once the site of a
cabin built in the 1940s. A fireplace mass rises from the existing stone outcropping.
Pivoting from this stone anchor, tiled roofs radiate about the hillside. The place is
characterized by stone ledges, an existing pine forest to the north of the forecourt, and a
heavy cedar log wall that wraps the southern edge. The house overlooks a mountainside
forest and a stream to the south. The site is reached from the northeast along an existing
drive that had been cut along the lower shoulder of the mountain. The stone ledge extends
into the house through the entry and under the log wall.*

*By using logs, heavy timbers, and stonework found in rustic buildings of the early 1900s
and arranging the new structure along the southern rim of the site, an evocative forespace
was created. . . . A log wall forms a veil between the forespace and the house, delaying
one's discovery of the landscape beyond. On the other side of the extended log wall is a
series of loosely arranged sheds that face the sun and overlook the valley, forest, and
stream below.*

*Entry through the shaded north wall reveals light and openness. Moving through the
house, the stone ledge twists around to the west, providing seating and the hearth for a
massive stone fireplace built of the same stone. . . . The staccato pattern of the roof
members is an expression of the stresses within the roof. In the spirit of older camp
structures, much of the framing for interior partitions and cabinets as well as galvanized
hardware and electrical fittings have been exposed to view adding to the visual richness of
this rural house.*

Employing a particular Pacific Northwest timber-framed syntax initially developed in association with James Cutler, this house demonstrates a level of carpentry work that is ever more rare today, craftsmanship having been in decline for over half a century. As such, it manifests a level of exposed timber construction that can stand comparison with some of the finest work produced by contemporary Japanese carpenters. At the same time, the skill deployed in the log wall and outriding structural frames is equal to the precision carpentry within, the overall prowess being particularly noticeable in the handling of the junction between the two systems, where the raftered eaves of the monopitched roofs project beyond the confines of the building to rest on the exterior log frames. This system is particularly evident in the massive cedar logs that carry the portico over the entry, the wall passing behind the trabeated frame before petering out into a stone ledge.

However unwittingly, this house is a casebook demonstration of German nineteenth-century theory, passing from Schopenhauer's famous discrimination between *stütze* and *last* (support and load) to Gottfried Semper's differentiation between "earthwork" and "roofwork" as lying at the very origin of all architecture, along with the hearth and the infill wall. In this house the salient role of the hearth and fireplace can hardly be missed nor can the focus they provide for the central living space, along with their embodiment in an undressed mass of stone. Here the allusion to Wright's Fallingwater (1937) is too direct to be denied, as is the way in which the building blends into the attendant landscape as though it had grown out of it.

Unlike Fallingwater, however, this house is a magnum opus of exposed timber construction, either milled or simply stripped, and it is this, along with the proliferation of strapped and bolted joints in galvanized metal, that give the house its unique character. At times this borders on over-articulation, as in the Japanese-esque detailing of the shelving in the study.

The Ledge House surely amounts to an unrepeatable moment for both
client and architect alike—a fact that is most poignantly expressed in
the diminutive suspension footbridge in core-ten steel that spans over
a nearby trout stream in the surrounding forest. One is reminded by
this feature of the primitive timber gate that leads into the attendant
woods from Alvar Aalto's Villa Mairea, completed in Noormarkku,
Finland, in 1939.

SR+T ARCHITECTS / KARLA ROTHSTEIN & JOEL TOWERS
ROSS HOUSE, 1995–1997

BALLSTON LAKE, SARATOGA, NEW YORK

This work, designed by two young architects at the very onset of their careers, may be seen as a diminutive masterwork in as much as the commission enabled them to demonstrate in a single work all they had learned during their graduate education, not only at the level of plan and section but also in terms of the sophistication they were able to bring to the detailing and construction of the house. The result also testifies to the faith of the clients, who still live in the house, given that they were willing to risk an unorthodox approach to their primary residence, situated on an idyllic site overlooking Ballston Lake, in Saratoga County, New York State. That the house was conceived as a sensitive but didactic exercise is confirmed by the architects' account of their initial intentions:

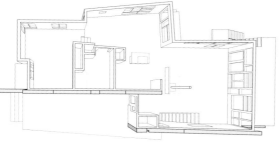

descending terrain, while asserting a strong leading edge off of which the volume and the program of the house unfold. *We carried these three elements—responsiveness to microclimate, landscape, and a clear reading of the structural and material character of the house—into a modern social and spatial context. The house attempts to negotiate continuity in the character of the local landscape with an emergent, modern sensibility.*

What is remarkable about this modest house is that its plan is almost an ideogram, consisting as it does of two precast, reinforced concrete spine walls slightly offset from each other but mutually embedded in the site like two parallel blades that descend a precipitous wooded slope toward the lake. Both of these walls are oriented east/west and where the one is anchored to the kitchen/bathroom core while extending eastward as a retaining wall to the ramped drive descending to the garage, the other, two stories in height, flanks the northern face of the stair hall leading to service facilities beneath. The gap between these two wall-planes accommodates a generous elevated terrace and entry from the east, whereupon one finds oneself in a high living room set before an equally generous veranda facing the lake.

Our design was shaped by a reflexive relationship between house and environment. The Adirondack summer camp style, comprised as it is of spacious overhung porches for sheltered outdoor summer living, from which residents retreat in winter in favor of centrally located dining and living rooms heated by wood burning stoves, informed the organization of this house. The topography of the site—a lightly wooded swath of land 615 feet (187 meters) long, that slopes from a rural road on the east to the lake front edge on the west, 70 feet (21 meters) below—drove our approach to the building and our decision to honor that landscape by constructing a roof-form that floats above the

Despite its elaborate sectional organization and the contrapuntal play with butterfly and monopitched roofs over different zones of the house, the bulk of the accommodation is on the main living level, which is subtly articulated in plan and section so as to create different "settings" in different sectors of what is essentially a single space. In this respect, the southern wall of the dining area is canted in such a way as to open toward a small balcony and a view of the lake beyond. The narrow end of the trapezoidal dining space leads directly to the only bedroom, which is raised some four steps above the datum of the living area. This subtle spatial organization stems from the placement of the central core, namely the kitchen/bathroom, the kitchen being planned in such a way as to serve with almost equal ease both the dining and the living space. In a parallel manner, the closed volume of the bathroom shields the bedroom from what would otherwise be a totally open plan. The rotary movement around the core is suggested by the position of the freestanding stove, together with its tubular metal chimney. A straight flight connects the living level to the lower ground floor, thereby affording access to the garage

and to an exercise room with a window onto the lake at the lower level. While isolating the garage from the living room, this stair also serves to access basement storage and laundry facilities.

The poetic character of this house, which from the exterior seems larger than it is, depends to a great degree on the contrast and interplay between two totally different modes of construction; on the one hand, the aforementioned precast concrete walls and, on the other, the wood framed, horizontal boarded construction typical of the region. The formal, technical, and conceptual interaction between these two tectonic modes has been lucidly characterized by the architects themselves:

The house is fabricated of sandblasted precast concrete panels, glass, and wood. The assembled precast concrete wall serves as an eccentric spine, supporting the floors as they reach to the eastern, southern, and western extents of the house. The material and spatial density of the precast concrete shelters the dwelling from the prevailing winds while its assembled mass grounds it to the site. The lightness of the glass and wood counterbalance the concrete, opening the house, in both plan and section, to the surrounding landscape.

Together the wood and concrete establish a hybrid, stable structure, while the glass and concrete create a dialectic of heavy and light, expanding toward the lake and sky.

The spine walls of the house were built up out of fourteen precast, prestressed concrete panels, each of a different shape and with different apertures, and each being seven inches thick, eight feet eight inches wide and assembled into position with a tower crane. Once each individual panel was hoisted into position, it was joined to the in situ concrete ground slab through metal plates already cast into the slab. The panels were then sandblasted to eliminate any superficial irregularities. In a subsequent phase, lower decks were poured, wooden floors were constructed, and the framed walls erected together with their roofs.

Among the most striking aspects of this work is the rhythmic character of the concrete walls, particularly as the taller of the two steps down the slope along with the seams between the panels. The syncopation of windows, large and small along the north elevation, contributes to this harmonic effect, as does the butterfly roof over the main volume projecting out toward the lake. The large overhangs of the roofs and the deep eaves give the building the profile of an oriental pavilion; this character is amplified by the timber fenestration and by the cedar boarding covering the east, south, and west elevations.

With the greatest subtlety, the architecture of Le Corbusier is a latent presence in this work as we may judge from the handling of the garage as though it were a "dock," which makes a reference to Le Corbusier's Maison Jaoul of 1956. The rhythmic fenestration of the north walls is equally indebted to Le Corbusier, only in this instance the reference is the Ronchamp chapel, which dates from the same period. Even the overhanging roof suggests the silhouette of Le Corbusier's unbuilt MAS-house prototype of 1940.

345

PATKAU ARCHITECTS
AGOSTA HOUSE,
1996–2000

SAN JUAN ISLAND, WASHINGTON

Built as an idyllic retirement home for a couple who had hitherto spent the best part of their working lives in New York City, this back-to-nature residence in the Pacific Northwest, near the Canadian border, is typical of the articulate syntax of the Vancouver-based practice of John and Patricia Patkau. The architects' description of this house is so concise and comprehensive as to merit quoting at some length:

The Agosta house sits in a grassy meadow enclosed on three sides by forty-three acres of second-growth Douglas fir forest. The fourth side of the meadows opens to the northwest, where it overlooks rolling fields and, across the Haro Strait in the distance, the Gulf

Islands of British Columbia. The house includes a separate structure with an office and guest quarters and also a vegetable and flower garden, which is protected from the numerous deer on San Juan Island by a twelve-foot-high fence.

The structure, which spans the ridge of the meadow, forms a "dam" that divides the site. An enclosed forecourt to the southeast suggests a spatial reservoir to be released through the house. . . . In section, walls and roofs are sloped to respond to the gentle but steady incline of the site. The organization of the house is the result of extruding and then manipulating this section, either by erosion, which produces exterior in-between spaces that divide the house programmatically, or by insertion, which uses ceiling bulkheads to separate the house's programmatic areas . . .

The construction of the house is simple in concept—a wood frame on a concrete slab. It is intended to have the direct quality of a rural or even agricultural building. The structure is a combination of exposed heavy timber framing and conventional stud-framing; most exterior surfaces are clad in light-gauge galvanized sheet steel, which protects the structure not only from the weather but from forest wildfires.

With its low profile, this single-story house is a layered spatial composition in which there are two main circulation routes: the first passes from the main entrance directly into the principal volume, which is separated into living and dining areas by a large, plastered chimney breast; the second is a separate informal approach that leads directly into the fenced garden and from there, via a covered walkway and a mudroom, into the kitchen. The kitchen, in turn, opens onto the dining area. Here, the two routes converge before leading out to the terrace overlooking the distant view. A separate subroute leads from the

covered walkway into the guest bedroom and an office/study space with its windows overlooking the garden court. The master bedroom/bathroom is located to the right of the main entry as a self-contained suite.

The concatenation of inclined planes that make up the horizontal body of the house—some tilted against the slope like the garden fence, some canting in the direction of the slope—jointly constitute the kind of a "spatial sluice" in which the inclined galvanized-sheet-steel walls, with upstand seams, have much the same character as the zinc-covered monopitched roofs and skylights covering the principal volumes; these also have standing seams, although they occur at double the module of the bounding walls. Thus, galvanized-steel wall planes at different depths, facing the mechanical room and the master bedroom respectively, stop short of each other so as to bracket the

main threshold into the house, where there is a suggestion of a view lying beyond the wood-framed entrance. One gleans a similar hint of a panorama lying beyond in the layering of the fence with horizontal louvers that flank the covered walk of the living room terrace. A fair-faced concrete ground slab cantilevers out over the site on the northwestern elevation, thereby giving the impression of levitation, of "touching the earth lightly," to coin the ecological slogan of Australian architect Glenn Murcutt.

As is often the case with North American houses, Frank Lloyd Wright is an omnipresent influence, this time for his tented Ocotillo Desert Camp, erected in 1927 on the Salt Range near Chandler, Arizona—the

overall horizontality of the camp stemming from timber battened screen walls and monopitched, canvas roofs stretched over triangulated timber frames. The boarded soffits of the deep eaves of the Agosta House are in contrast to the overall galvanized silver gray tone of the house, including the tongued and grooved external boarding of the return walls that run at right angles to the inclined frontal planes. Closed on the southwest and northeast elevations, the house opens up as a light modulator to the diurnal play of eastern and western light. Finally one should note that all too stoically, given the rainy climate, the carport is removed from the house in the surrounding forest, meaning that owners and visitors alike must approach the house on foot across the open meadow.

ZOKA ZOLA
PFANNER HOUSE, 1997–2002

CHICAGO, ILLINOIS

This brick-clad, timber-framed four-story house, built on a corner lot in the Ukrainian Village area of Chicago, is a subtly contextual response to the densely packed urban fabric in which it is situated. As a result it recalls something of the British brutalist brick aesthetic of the mid-

1950s. At the same time its spatial vivacity and refinement ensures that there is nothing lugubrious or somber about its spirit. Built tight against the sidewalk on its northern and western edges, this orthogonal work induces a series of countervailing inflections vectoring first this way and

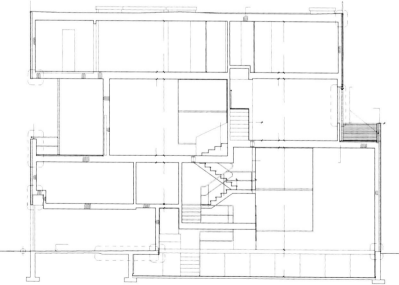

then that from the western and eastern ends of its narrow megaronlike form. A primary aspect of this inflection is the play between large and more moderately sized windows that interact with subtle planar recesses in the brick skin, which is otherwise opaque throughout. Despite the homogeneity of the brick revetment with its matching mortar, the size and the position of the fenestration is such as to afford unexpected views over the flanking streets, and this extroversion extends even to the bedroom level where it affords a sweeping, panoramic vista over the roofs of the adjoining houses that make up the rest of the block.

The key to the spatial dynamism of this house is the open stair, which the visitor encounters immediately on entering the house through the northern elevation. Here there is little by way of a threshold in the conventional sense, since one finds oneself on a fairly narrow causeway overlooking the architect's office, which is recessed almost a half-story below grade. Aside from being the initial landing of a stair from which one accesses the architect's office below or the library above, this promenade serves as a potential route between the garage at the eastern end and the garden situated to the west.

In the analysis the essential *parti* of this house turns on the interlock between two switchback stairs, with the upper stair, running east/west, connecting the library to the living room, as opposed to the lower stair, which crosses the section from north to south. It is just this counter-change in the direction of the going of the stair that enables the architect to enter each successive floor at an appropriate point in the plan. Thus one enters the living room via a stair rising from east to west, only to turn around completely and gain access to the kitchen-dining space via a shorter stair rising from west to east, the space flowing through the stair. On attaining this level, the stair changes direction once more in order to transverse across the section to afford access to the bedroom level above. This final "knight's move," so to speak, involves cantilevering a landing as a crow's nest on top of the house affording a double symmetrical mode of access to the master bedroom suite to the west, along with a small guest room and an ample child's room to the east, coupled with an adjoining bathroom and built-in laundry facilities.

In the spirit of Gaston Bachelard's elegiac text *The Poetics of Space*, this house abounds in the action settings that are delicately tuned to the life of the occupants. One begins on the ground floor with an overview of the office that acquires its spaciousness not only from being recessed below grade but also from the slightly displaced picture windows that not only open to the street but also receive southern light from a narrow alley to the rear of the house. From this

357

setting one passes to the low-ceilinged intimacy of the library with its incidental square windows, before passing to the living room above.

Via a full-height sliding door, this last gives onto an ample balcony that is spatially inflected toward the corner where bounding streets intersect. This feature is countered by a discrete fireplace in the opposite corner (the only hearth in the house) together with reading niche incorporated into the upstand masonry that completes the southwest corner. A reciprocal of this inflected arrangement occurs in the dining room/terrace sequence together with a built-in stainless steel kitchen that follows around the opposing corner fenestration at the southeast corner of the volume. This stainless steel surface is offset by light wooden cabinetry lining the re-entrant corner, thereby imparting a sense of occasion appropriate to formal dining.

A similar precision animates and enriches the master bedroom suite, from the long panoramic window facing out over the adjoining roofscape to a narrow skylight set directly above the head of the double bed. A continuous loop of circulation links the bedroom to the dressing room/bathroom sequence before returning to the bedroom once more. This overall size of spatial fluidity is enhanced by the full-height doors separating the guest and master sleeping spaces.

The philosophical credo underlying the overall rhythmic arrangement of this house has been amply enlarged upon by the architect:

How can that house not trap us in? As an architect of my own house how is it possible not to be housed inside my own limits? How can we let time run its own delightful progression? This house is designed not to feel owned. When the building feels owned it's impoverished, because it has a flattened relationship with the rest of the world. How are the ideas of wanting to impress others and representation reconciled? The guest and the host of the house are treated equally in this house. The guest washroom is a place where the guest feels alone in the center of the house, having privacy to contemplate it. Which parts of our interiors to make public is our dilemma. This house is not exposing its intimacy but its interior, so that other people can inhabit it as part of their own mental space, rather than observe the intimate life of its owners. The landscape we'll see through the windows of the house is not purely visual and not framed selectively according to the ideas of good view, instead it is a reminder of what is there in its proximity. Not the same space or a community but the proximity . . . The terrace is the main space of pleasure. The bodily pleasure, social pleasure, pleasures with passage of time, pleasure with air, sun, and trees. The kitchen counter and the balcony and the bathrooms are the places of pleasure of daily activity. At the exits from the house, entrances, balcony extension, terrace, and the bedroom extension are the only places of daily pleasure of being with the house.

RICK JOY
TYLER HOUSE, 2000
TUBAC, ARIZONA

Situated in the Arizona desert some fifty miles south of Tucson and approximately the same distance from the Mexican border, this house was built as a retirement home for an Ohio businessman and his wife, who happen to share a mutual enthusiasm for astronomy—a passion that may be most advantageously pursued in the clear night air of the desert. Carefully laid into a declivity and bounded by a continuous concrete retaining wall, this dwelling is divided into two separate freestanding elements by a reinforced concrete stair that leads down into a common forecourt serving both units. The single-story larger wing of the house is a twenty-five-hundred-square-foot living volume with a high monopitched roof. This is clearly separated from a fifteen-hundred-square-foot two-story wing that accommodates a garage, a large workshop, and two guest bedrooms.

Both units are faced in rusting sheet steel and covered by equally rusty monopitched corrugated iron roofs. The two orthogonal wings focus on a common terrace and swimming pool, which curtails the composition at the western end of a central patio. Of this composition, subtly influenced by the domestic work of Luis Barragán and Glenn Murcutt, Rick Joy has written: "*The house's weathered steel forms, like some rusted artifacts from a cowboy camp, are oriented to frame prime views. The coarseness of the rough steel exterior contrasts with the refinement of the interior palette of white plaster, stainless steel, maple and translucent glass.*"

Of more consequence than the small areas of opalescent glass is the large, mullionless window-wall of gasketed plate glass that bounds the

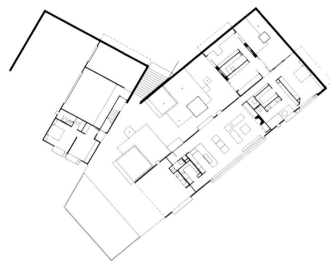

large living/dining/kitchen volume to the south, thereby affording the main living space panoramic views over the Tumacori mountain range visible in the distance. Set at angles to each other, the main house, L-shaped in plan, combines with the ancillary wing to enclose an entry forecourt, which is articulated by steel-tanked reflecting pools and by cacti and other desert shrubs. A subtle reciprocity is set up in the forecourt between the plate-glass, flush-glazed projecting window of the living room, framed in steel plate, and an adjacent reflecting pool, also framed in steel, where the water brought to the rim of the tank serves as a horizontal mirror image of the plate-glass bay window.

The amenities provided by the main house are completed at the western end by a terrace, shielded from the sun on three sides by the overrun of the roof and the side walls. At the opposing eastern end, the living room leads directly into the master bedroom/dressing/bathroom suite and, at one side, to separate offices for the husband and wife overlooking the forecourt; both the master bedroom and the access corridor are enriched by views over the patio. In contrast, the terrace at the southern end of the main house terminates the composition with a poolside terrace-cum-belvedere overlooking the infinite expanse of the desert beyond.

Discreetly integrated into the topography, this house constantly changes its total image depending on the vantage point from which it is approached. Thus, while it appears as a monumental hangar when viewed from the pool, it assumes a much more lateral and linear monopitched form when approached from the south, the north, or the southeast; the rusty steel revetment contrasts with the gray concrete retaining walls, bounded at a middle distance by an irregular field of barrel cacti. All of this returns us, by association, to the defensive character of the core-ten revetment which, attached by rivets to the cast concrete walls of the house, bows slightly between its vertical seams so as to evoke the ruined techniques of another era, a crippled tank or beached dreadnought inexplicably stranded in an inhospitable desert to form the basis of an unlikely dwelling. The thin line of oversailing corrugated eaves and the rusted stove-pipe chimneys and roof-top ventilators only serve to augment this image of a latterday stockade.

BARTON AND VICKI MYERS
HOUSE AND STUDIO, 2001

TORO CANYON, MONTECITO,
CALIFORNIA

Influenced by the Southern Californian, Spanish Colonial tradition and by the canonical house that Charles and Ray Eames built for themselves in Pacific Palisades, Los Angeles, in 1958, this house and studio, erected on a steeply sloping site in Toro Canyon, is a tour de force in prefab rationalized assembly. Predicated on an exposed skeleton steel frame with stanchions at twenty-foot intervals, the initial economy of this residential compound derives from the fact that its trabeated structure was fabricated off-site out of welded, precut standard sections. These components were shipped to the site and erected on the three concrete platforms stepping up the slope that accommodate, in sequence, the guest house, the main house, and the studio. Each of these single-story steel-framed structures was roofed with standard steel decking, while the floor-to-ceiling height varied from nine feet in the guest house to sixteen feet in the residential and studio units.

Stepping up the slope and facing south toward the ocean and the distant Channel Islands, each pavilion is equipped with a deep, cantilevered overhang projecting over the adjacent terrace. The fairly wide spacing of the units, the deployment of insulated roll-down steel shutters over every window, and the permanent covering of the roofs of both the house and studio with shallow pools of water, were all moves designed to minimize the exposure to damage by fire. Despite their size these shutters are easily operated manually, so that the entire house may be rapidly shut down in case of a wildfire. Save for the modified chain boxes these shutters are standard, as are the glazed up-and-over garage doors that enable the main spaces to be opened up fully to the exterior. Since there are no mosquitoes and other bothersome insects on the upper slopes of the canyon the house can be left open and naturally ventilated 75 percent of the time, year-round.

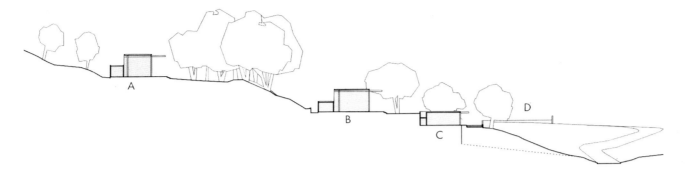

The whole complex may be seen as proto-ecological not only because the structural frame was made out of recycled steel but also because the site was carefully terraced, channeled, and planted with vetiver grass, cacti, and ground cover, so as to stabilize the soil and control the water runoff. Further to this the oaks flanking the compound were sensitively thinned by felling to retard fire spread.

The principal residential unit (B) is divided into servant and served volumes in as much as the twenty-five-by-thirty-eight-foot living/dining area and the twenty-five-by-twenty-foot kitchen are jointly attended by a parallel wing having a lower floor-to-ceiling height. This wing accommodates a master bedroom and a guest bedroom at either end accompanied by separate master and guest bathrooms/dressing suites situated in proximity to the units they serve. Between these two sets there is a separate bathroom and an auxiliary room opening off a service corridor, appropriately divided by a door into master and guest sleeping quarters.

The studio (A), situated higher up the slope, is of the same structural module and consequently of the same floor area and height as the main living/dining volume. Moreover, it is similarly zoned with a servant, archival area to the rear of the studio. The northern walls of the servant zones in each of the three buildings are made of insulated in situ reinforced concrete construction while the flanking eastern and western elevations are equipped with full-height sliding windows. Concrete chimney shafts are planted in the center of these return facades, serving double-sided fireplaces at the ends of each unit.

There is something decidedly Wrightian about the way in which this three-part composition steps up from one terrace to the next as the complex climbs up the slope. This is in no small measure due to the overhangs and to the way in which the glazed up-and-over doors recall the proportions of Wright's textile block houses. Access to the main house is by a stair leading directly up from a three-car garage and driveway situated at the base of the complex, adjacent to the guest suite (C), which has its own terrace, bathroom, and kitchen.

In the last analysis the *parti* of this house derives from the particularities of the site, not only the ecological fragility of the landscape but also the perennial risks of fire and earthquakes. Hence the fundamental principle adopted at the very beginning of the design process—namely, to divide the house into discrete units so as to minimize the environmental impact of each unit and enhance the natural beauty of the environment.

MICHAEL BELL
GEFTER/PRESS RESIDENCE, 2007

GHENT, NEW YORK

Built in the midst of a partially cleared copse on a site with a slight fall from north to south, this completely glazed, single-story house may be readily characterized as neo-Miesian. However, it departs in subtle ways from the Miesian canon in order to set up a series of planar inflections that are more syncopated and layered in character than the trabeated dematerialized form of, say, Mies van der Rohe's Farnsworth House, by which it has surely been influenced. Familiarly known as the "binocular" house, this dwelling comprises three basic elements: a large kitchen/dining/living volume (forty by twenty feet) that links two separate bedroom/study wings of different lengths.

In general, the basic structure consists of four-by-four-inch stanchions supporting twelve-by-four-inch hollow steel beams or channels, with the overall frame being site-welded into position. A standard twelve-by-four-inch steel fascia is variously employed from one segment of the perimeter to the next, while variations occur in the positioning of the glass skin from one sector to the next. This skin is usually carried in front of the stanchion line or, in the instance of the long span over the south face of the living room, it is set behind it. This planar layering in glass is reinforced as an abstract relief by the alternately black and white finish to the window/door frames that is adopted

consistently throughout. The doors are painted white and fixed glass framing is painted black to match the black of the steel fascias and the black solid steel panel of the entry door to the living volume.

This kind of syncopation is continued in the various concrete earthworks that anchor the dematerialized structure into its site—in the first instance, with the external concrete causeway, the datum and width of which mirrors the internal concrete corridor serving the bedroom/study wing. This causeway is inseparable from the concrete apron that grounds the elevations of the courtyard, at the same datum,

and eventually terminates in a fourteen-by-ten-foot terrace at the end of the study wing. A dwarf wall in concrete, the same height as the podium, extends from the internal corridor into the ground, settling the building into the contours of the site.

The further syncopated details pertain to the house considered as a relief construction and in this regard merit our attention. The first and the more spatial of these are the delicate metal pergolas that parallel the southwestern faces of the two attendant wings and are meant to carry canvas awnings in high summer in order to protect the more

vulnerable elevations of the house. The second is the variation
between channels and hollow steel fascias, with the architect
employing the former for the long facades and reserving the latter for
short return faces. Minimal overrun at the corners between these
fascias suggests a rotation in the overall form while the pergolas imply
a countermanding frontality. These ephemeral pergolas engender a
perspectival reading that is countered by ever-changing oblique views
across the U-shaped figure of the plan, thereby proliferating reflective
surfaces, spatial layerings, and multiple framings of both the house
and its wooden environment. Unlike other canonical glass houses, to
which its chromium-plate tubular-steel furnishings are obviously
indebted, the Binocular House, with its sliding glass walls, is
conceived as a pavilion that may be opened up in summer to the
landscape on all sides. At the same time its double glazing and precise
insulation, along with its sophisticated heating systems, assure its
year-round role as a weekend retreat.

INTRODUCTION NOTES

FROM THE BROWN DECADES TO THE FRAGMENTED METROPOLIS, 1869–1929

1. Vincent Scully, *Modern Architecture* (New York: Braziller, 1965) 18.

2. Henry-Russell Hitchcock, *The Architecture of H. H. Richardson and His Times* (Hamden, Conn: Archon Books, 1961) 268.

3. Grant Carpenter Manson, *Frank Lloyd Wright to 1910* (New York: Van Nostrand Reinhold, 1958) 39.

4. Frank Lloyd Wright, "Modern Architecture: The Kahn lectures" 1931, see *Frank Lloyd Wright: Collected Writings, Vol. 2, 1930–1932* (New York: Rizzoli, 1992) 8.

5. Frank Lloyd Wright, *An Autobiography* (London: Longmans, Green & Co., 1932) 235.

SURVIVAL THROUGH DESIGN: THE TRIUMPH OF THE MODERN AMERICAN HOUSE, 1929–1945

1. Thomas Hines, *Richard Neutra and the Search for Modern Architecture* (New York: Oxford University Press, 1982) 120. Hines refers to the Beard House as being "all metal."

2. Grace Miller taught the Mensendieck system of functional excercise. See Hines, 121.

3. *Richard Neutra Buildings and Projects* (Zurich: Ginsberger, 1951) 38.

4. Commissioned in 1936, largely on the basis of Neutra's already substantial reputation, Windshield was built for John Nicholas Brown of Rhode Island. This very large house erected on Fisher's Island, New York, was in fact built twice; first completed in April 1938, it was destroyed in the hurricane that struck the East Coast in the fall of that year. It was then rebuilt with modifications and reopened in 1939. Brown's wife rather facetiously suggested that the name should be changed to "Won't Shield." See Thomas Hines, *Richard Neutra and the Search for the Modern Architecture*, 158.

5. *Richard Neutra and the Search for the Modern Architecture*, 50.

6. Henry Plummer, *The Potential House*. (Special issue of the magazine *A+U, Tokyo*), September 1986, 126.

7. Esther McCoy, *The Second Generation* (Salt Lake City: Peregrine Smith Books, 1984) 157.

8. Esther McCoy, *The Second Generation*, 15.

BLUEPRINT FOR MODERN LIVING: THE AMERICAN HOUSE AND THE PAX AMERICANA, 1945–1965

1. Frederick Kiesler, *Inside the Endless House: Art, People and Architecture: A Journal* (New York: Simon & Schuster, 1966).

2. Robert Stern, *New Directions in American Architecture* (new enlarged edition) (New York: Braziller, 1977) 71.

3. John Lautner, "Meet the Architect," *GA Houses*, 32, July 1991, 32.

4. See Paul Heyer, *Conversation with Architects* 114.

COMPLEXITY AND CONTRADICTION: THE LATE-MODERN HOUSE, 1965–2007

1. Robert Venturi, *Complexity and Contradiction in Architecture* (New York: The Museum of Modern Art, 1966) 106–107.

2. Vincent Scully, *The Shingle Style Today or The Historian's Revenge* (New York: Braziller, 1974) 36–37.

3. Clive Bamford Smith, *Builders in the Sun: Five Mexican Architects* (New York: Architectural Book Publishing Co., 1967) 54.

4. Batey & Mack, *GA Houses*, 10 (1982) 94.

5. *GA Architect 11* (A.D.A. Editor Tokyo 1993) 66.

6. Frank Israel, "Architecture: E. Fay Jones," *Architectural Digest 35* (1978): 79.

7. Philip Arcidi, "A Desert Lookout," *Progressive Architecture* (November 1990) 76.

PHOTO CREDITS